The Middle East and the West

BERNARD LEWIS

HARPER TORCHBOOKS
Harper & Row, Publishers
New York, Hagerstown, San Francisco, London

THE MIDDLE EAST AND THE WEST

Copyright © 1964 by Bernard Lewis

Printed in the United States of America.

This book was first published in 1964, by Indiana University Press, Bloomington, Indiana. It is here reprinted by arrangement.

First HARPER TORCHBOOK edition published 1966 by
Harper & Row, Publishers, Incorporated
10 East 53rd Street
New York, New York 10022.

Library of Congress Catalog Card No.: 64–10830

79 10 9

CONTENTS

PREFACE

THIS book contains the text of six public lectures, delivered at Indiana University, Bloomington, between March 19 and April 23, 1963. Their theme is the relations between the Middle East and the West – the impact of both Western action and Western civilization on the Islamic peoples and societies of the Middle East, and the successive phases of Middle Eastern response. In the first chapter I have attempted to define the Middle East as an historical, geographical, and cultural entity; in the second, to show what the West has meant and means to Middle Easterners, and to trace the processes of Western intrusion, influence, domination, and partial withdrawal. The next three chapters deal with political and intellectual movements in the Middle East in recent and modern times, in three main groups – liberal and socialist, patriotic and nationalist, Islamic. The final chapter examines the place and role of the countries of the Middle East in international affairs, and concludes with a consideration of some of the factors affecting Western policy toward them.

I should like to record my thanks to Indiana University for giving me this opportunity to present my views on this subject, and to my colleagues and students at Bloomington for their gracious and friendly hospitality during the six weeks of my stay. My thanks are also due to my colleagues Dr S. A. A. Rizvi and Dr M. E. Yapp, for several helpful suggestions, and to Professor A. T. Hatto and Mr E. Kedourie for reading and criticizing my typescript. They are of course in no way responsible for any defects that remain. Finally, I would like to thank Professor W. Cantwell Smith and the New American Library of World Literature Inc., for permission to reproduce the passage cited on p. 112 and Simon and Schuster for a quotation from James G. McDonald's *My Mission to Israel*.

School of Oriental and African Studies,   B.L.
University of London,
June, 1963.

CHAPTER I

Sketches for an Historical Portrait

THE term Middle East was invented in 1902 by the American naval historian Alfred Thayer Mahan, to designate the area between Arabia and India, with its centre – from the point of view of the naval strategist – in the Persian Gulf. This new geographical expression was taken up by *The Times* and later by the British Government, and, together with the slightly earlier term 'Near East', soon passed into general use. Both names are recent but not modern; both are relics of a world with Western Europe in the centre, and other regions grouped around it. Yet in spite of their obsolete origin and parochial outlook both terms, 'Middle East' in particular, have won universal acceptance, and are now used to designate this region even by Russians, Africans, and Indians, for whom in fact it lies south, north, or west – even, strangest of all, by the peoples of the Middle East themselves. So useful has the term been found that the area of its application, as well as of its use, has been vastly extended – from the original coastlands of the Persian Gulf to a broad region stretching from the Black Sea to equatorial Africa and from India to the Atlantic.[1]

It is indeed remarkable that a region of such ancient civilization – the most ancient in the world – should have come to be known, even to itself, by names that are so new and so colourless. Yet, if we try to find an adequate substitute for these names we shall have great difficulty. In India the attempt has indeed been made to displace the Western-centred term Middle East by another, and the area has been renamed 'Western Asia'. This new geographical expression has rather more shape and colour than 'Middle East', but is not really very much better. It is no less misleading to view the region as the West of an entity called Asia than as the Middle East of another

9

unspecified entity; moreover it is improper to designate it by a name which, even formally, excludes Egypt.

The reason for the rapid spread and acceptance of the terms Near and Middle East must be sought in the fact that for Europeans this region was, for millennia, *the* East – the classical, archetypal and immemorial orient which has been the neighbour and rival of Greco-Roman and Christian Europe from the days when the armies of the Great King of Persia first invaded the lands of the Greeks until the days when the last rearguards of the Ottoman Sultans withdrew. Well into the nineteenth century, the countries of SW Asia and NE Africa were, for the European, still simply The East, without any need for closer specification, and the problem of their disposal was the Eastern Question. It was only when Europe became involved in the problems of a vaster and remoter orient that a closer definition became necessary. When the Far East began to concern the chanceries of Europe, some separate designation of the nearer east was needed. The term Near East was originally applied, in the late nineteenth century, to that part of south-eastern Europe that was then still under Turkish rule. It was 'Near' because it was, after all, Christian and European; it was 'East' because it was still under the rule of the Ottoman Empire – of an Islamic and oriental state. For a while the Near East was, so to speak, extended eastward, and, especially in American usage, came to embrace the greater part of the territories of the Ottoman Empire, in Asia and Africa as well as in Europe. In British usage – perhaps because on closer acquaintance the Near East proved less near than had at first been thought – the term Near East has almost disappeared, and has been replaced by a vastly extended Middle East, covering large areas of SW Asia and North Africa. There is still considerable variation in the usage of the latter term.

In spite of its recent emergence and of a continuing uncertainty as to its precise location, the term Middle East does nevertheless designate an area with an unmistakable character and identity, a distinctive – and familiar – personality shaped by strong geographical features and by a long and famous history.

The most striking geographical characteristic of the Middle East is certainly its aridity – the vast expanses of waste-land in almost every part of it. Rainfall is sparse, forests are few, and, except for a few privileged areas, agriculture depends on perennial irrigation, and requires constant defence against natural and human erosion. Most of the Arabian peninsula, apart from its south-western and south-eastern corners, consists of desert – the Fertile Crescent is little more than a rim of irrigable and cultivable land around its northern edges. Egypt too is nearly all desert, save only for the green gash of the Nile, opening out into the Delta towards the shore of the Mediterranean Sea. Much of North Africa is now infertile, except for the coastal belt and a few oases. In Turkey and Persia much of the central plateaux consists of desert and steppe, while beyond them, to the north, lie the vast steppe-lands of Eurasia.

Some of the deserts, as in the Empty Quarter of Arabia and the Western Desert of Egypt, are utterly barren; others support a thin but historically important population of nomadic herdsmen, who provide animals for meat and transport, and participate, in various ways, in the exploitation of the trans-desert trade-routes. In modern times the herdsmen are losing an important part of their economic *raison d'être*, as horse and camel are replaced by car and lorry – mounts which they are unable to breed. They can however feed them, and in some areas they and their neighbours are supplied with vast quantities of the fodder which these mounts consume. The exploitation of these resources – of petroleum – is bringing social as well as economic changes of incalculable scope and extent.

Between the herdsmen and the tillers of the soil there is an ancient feud. One of the earliest records of the conflict between them is contained in some verses of the fourth chapter of the book of Genesis, which tells of the quarrel of Abel, the stock-raiser, and Cain, the farmer. In the Bible it is Cain who kills Abel; more frequently in the history of the Middle East it has been the herdsmen who killed the peasants, or established their rule over them. The policing of the desert borders and the security of the desert trade-routes were always problems for the governments, whether local or imperial, that controlled the settled country. They usually found it more convenient to deal with the desert by indirect means – through some sort of nomadic or oasis principality to which they gave support and recognition in return for commercial facilities and for political and military help when required. To take one example among many: Byzantium and Persia, the two world powers that confronted one another across the Middle East in the sixth century, both maintained their Arabian buffer-states, whose rulers they encouraged with gifts of gold and of weapons, with high-sounding titles, and with visits to the imperial capital. This method was cheaper, easier, and more effective than trying to rule the desert directly. Its merits are in no way diminished by the fact that in the seventh century the Arabs came out of the desert and overwhelmed both of them.

Conquest from the desert is a recurring theme in the history of the Middle East. Many waves of invasion, of migration and of settlement, have burst into the cultivated lands. Some, like those of the Accadians, the Canaanites, the Aramaeans and the Hebrews in antiquity, were of Semitic peoples from the Arabian wilderness; others came southward from the steppe-lands of central, northern and eastern Asia. The last and greatest of the Semitic invasions was that of the Muslim Arabs in the seventh century, which inaugurated medieval Islamic civilization; the greatest of the steppe invasions was that of the Mongols in the thirteenth century, who, in the judgment of some historians, ended it.

The immediate impact of the Mongol conquests was certainly great; their subsequent effects have been much exaggerated. At one time, Mongol brutality was blamed for the decline of Islamic civilization and, indeed, for all the failings of the Middle East and its peoples between the thirteenth and nineteenth centuries. Outside romantic and apologetic circles, this view has been generally abandoned, as increased knowledge of Islamic history on the one hand, and closer experience of brutality and destruction on the other, have shown us that the damage done by the Mongols was neither as great nor as lasting as it seemed to historians of a more innocent age than our own. The Mongols did not destroy Arab civilization, which was advanced in decay long before they appeared; nor did they destroy Islamic civilization, which, in a predominantly Persianized form, achieved a new flowering under their rule.

But Islamic civilization, though not destroyed, was undoubtedly transformed by the coming of the steppe peoples.

The great migrations of these peoples into the Middle East had begun before the Mongol conquests, in the tenth century, when the Turkish tribes of Central Asia crossed the Jaxartes and began their march of conquest westwards. They ended in the period after the death of Tamerlane, the last of the great steppe conquerors, in 1405. During these four centuries of invasion and domination from the steppe, the whole pattern of life and government in the Middle East was changed.

Thereafter there were no more invasions from the desert or the steppe. When the Wahhābīs in eighteenth century Arabia, moved by a new religious fervour and a new expansionist drive, tried to emulate the feats of their ancestors by invading Syria and Iraq, they were stopped on the desert borders and hurled back. The Ottoman Empire, then in the last stages of decrepitude, succeeded with ease where the mighty empires of Rome and Persia had failed. The difference was, of course, the technological superiority of the larger power over the smaller, which began with the advent of the first firearm and has been growing ever since. The Persian and Byzantine armies faced the desert invaders with weapons little, if at all, better than those of their enemies; the Ottomans stopped them with guns.

Here and there the desert is broken by rivers, which can be used for irrigation. Two of the most important countries, Egypt and Iraq, are essentially river valleys. Both have societies of great antiquity – certainly the most ancient in the area, probably in the world. Both have agrarian economies based on elaborate artificial irrigation, using the flood water of the rivers, and requiring large numbers of workers and of skilled technicians, controlled by a central administrative authority. This need determined the evolution of the system of land tenure; it also encouraged the growth of strong, centralized governments, at once bureaucratic and autocratic, and of a corresponding tradition of political thought and behaviour. Egypt and Iraq have for millennia been rival centres of power, and their modes of thought and organization have profoundly influenced the neighbouring countries. It was from these centres that civilization first arose and spread in the Middle East, in remote antiquity; in these centres again that, after the long eclipse from Cyrus to Muhammad, the new imperial civilization of Islam was born and grew to greatness. Since the Middle Ages

Egypt has, by superior numbers and economic resources, decisively outstripped Iraq, though the wealth accruing to the latter from oil sometimes obscures the growing inequality.

Egypt and Iraq have not always been the rival masters of the Middle East. There have been other centres of power in the area, the seats of empires which for long periods dominated the more ancient lands. North and east of the plains and valleys that make up the Fertile Crescent lie the great, high plateaux of Iran and Anatolia, clearly marked off from them in geographical configuration, in population, in cultural tradition, and in political experience. These lands were profoundly influenced by the Semitic civilizations of the Fertile Crescent, both in their ancient and their Islamic flowerings. But though they have passed through many ethnic and linguistic changes and adopted several Semitic scripts, they never adopted Semitic speech. Persians in the east, Hittites, Greeks and Turks in the north, have stood on roughly the same ethnic boundaries. Ottomans and Safavids in the sixteenth century resumed the roles and conflicts of Byzantines and Sasanids in the sixth, and evoked still more ancient memories. Today the tablelands form the two states of Turkey and Persia, inhabited by peoples who, though Muslim, share neither the language of the Arabs, nor the long trauma of subjection and liberation. The dividing-line between Arab and non-Arab is an old one; the frontier which it marks, along the foothills and the mountain approaches, is very much older.

Between Taurus and Sinai, between the desert and the sea, lie the four modern states of Syria, Lebanon, Israel and Jordan, which the Romans called Syria and Palestine, the Arabs called the lands of Shām, and European traders called the Levant. The broken terrain of this region is in marked contrast with the river valleys and plateaux which supported the neighbouring empires, and has usually been reflected in a cultural and political fragmentation. Only on rare occasions has the temporary eclipse of other powers permitted the emergence of a strong power in Syria; more often, the Syrian lands formed a mosaic of small principalities, the objects and the scene of struggles between their more powerful neighbours. When the rulers of Egypt were strong, it was they who tried to extend their control into as much of Palestine and Syria as possible – as did Pharaoh Thutmosis and Ptolemy, Pompey and Ibn Ṭūlūn, Fatimids and Mamluks, Napoleon, Muḥammad ʿAlī and the British. Egypt is most vulnerable on her north-eastern frontier, through which so many invaders have come, and Egyptian governments have usually tried to maintain at least a bridgehead on the far side of Sinai. At other times the Levant was dominated from the east – as by the Assyrians, the Persians and the Abbasids; from the north – as by the Hittites, Byzantines and Ottomans; or from the sea.

A dominant geographical feature of this region is the spine of mountains that runs down its centre – the Lebanon and Anti-Lebanon, with their northward and southward extensions. It divides the Syrian lands into two – a western slope, facing the Mediterranean and Europe, and an eastern slope facing the desert and Asia. The distinction between them is an old one, and has from time to time been renewed by fresh waves of invasion from both sides. The Philistines and the Phoenicians were both sea-peoples, the former coming from the West, the latter facing towards it; the ancient Israelites were a people of the desert and the hills, who held and finally defeated the Philistine invaders. Greek and Roman culture flourished in the coastlands, and languished in the interior. Antioch was a great Greek metropolis, and the maritime city of Berytus housed a notable school of Roman law – the Roman university of Beirut, as it were. Only occasionally, as under the Maccabees in Judea, did the older culture of the interior assert itself against the pervasive Hellenistic influence. The Arab invasions renewed the hegemony of the East, and for a brief interval even made Damascus an imperial capital. The Crusaders, marching south from Antioch to Gaza, for a while restored the Levant coast to Europe, but could not penetrate the interior. They never entered Aleppo or Damascus, and were only able to hold Jerusalem, their main objective, for a short time. In our own day, the distinction between the two is still clear – as between Beirut and Damascus, or, in a quite different and very much more acute form, between Tel Aviv and Amman.

A hundred and fifty years ago, when the European science of Egyptology was just beginning, all that was known of the ancient Middle East, before the conquests of Alexander, was what was said about it by the Bible and the Greek authors.

There were still Egyptians in Egypt, Persians in Persia, the descendants of other ancient peoples in neighbouring lands; but the old states and religions and civilizations were dead and literally buried, the old languages long since forgotten, their secrets locked in ancient scripts that no one could decipher. Only two of the peoples active in the ancient Middle East had survived with a continuing identity and memory. The Greeks and Jews were still Greeks and Jews, and still knew Greek and Hebrew; in these ancient yet living languages they had preserved immortal works of religion and literature, which passed into the common inheritance of mankind. In these works was all that the living memory of man had retained of the ancient Middle East. Even that much was barely known among the Muslims, who read neither the Bible nor the Greek historians, and had only a little second-hand information, filtered through from these same sources, together with a few vague legends of uncertain origin. The rediscovery of the ancient Middle East was wholly the work of European scholarship – of archaeologists who found the sources of information, philologists who deciphered and interpreted them, of historians and others who evaluated and exploited them. Their scholarship ultimately found disciples in the Middle East, and added a new dimension to the historical self-awareness of its peoples, which had hitherto in effect been limited to the period beginning with the Islamic revelation.

The Middle East is the home of three great religions, Judaism, Christianity, and Islam. All three of them still survive there; one has prevailed. For the last thirteen and a half centuries the Middle East has been pre-eminently the land of Islam, the geographical and spiritual centre of the Islamic world, where the Muslim faith was born and where the civilization of Islam received its first, classical formulations. Islam is by no means limited to the Middle East. There are vast communities of Muslims in Africa and Asia, some of them far larger than the combined population of the Middle East. But all of them are secondary, post-classical, in a sense colonial, related to the heartlands of Islam as are the lands of overseas settlement to Europe. It was in the Middle East that the great events took place which form the common historical memory of Muslims everywhere, and that the classic Islamic identity evolved; it was there that the basic Islamic patterns and traditions took shape, in the dominions of the caliphs and sultans of the great universal empires of medieval Islam, in lands that were predominantly of Arabic, Persian, and Turkish speech.

Since the rise of Islam in the seventh century, these three languages have predominated in the region, ousting such earlier media of communication and culture as Greek, Coptic and Syriac, and condemning them either to extinction or to liturgical or dialectal fossilization. The three are very unlike one another, belonging to different and unrelated language families. Arabic is a Semitic language, akin to Hebrew and Syriac; Persian an Indo-European language, related to Sanskrit on the one side and to most of the languages of Europe on the other; Turkish belongs to another group again, the Turco-Tatar family of languages, extending across Central Asia to the Far East and even to the Arctic. The three languages, though structurally quite different, are culturally closely related; an immense vocabulary of Arabic loanwords is used by Persian, and of Arabic and Persian loanwords by Turkish. Persians and Turks alike drew on Arabic as Europeans drew on Latin and Greek, both to borrow existing terms for old notions, and to coin new terms for new ones. 'Metaphysics' and 'telegraphy' are both English words of Greek etymology; the Arabic vocabulary of Turkish offers parallels to both types of borrowing.

The peoples who spoke these three languages appeared successively in the centre of the Middle Eastern stage. The first were the Arabs. At the beginning of the seventh century the Arabs were to be found only in the Arabian peninsula and its borderlands. The many countries in South West Asia and North Africa which are now called Arab were inhabited by a variety of nations, most of them Christians by religion, some but not all Semitic in speech. They spoke numerous languages –Aramaic in the Fertile Crescent, Coptic in Egypt, Berber and neo-Punic in North Africa; in addition, they used Greek in the East and Latin in the West as media of government, commerce, and culture.

As a result of the successive waves of conquest and colonization which followed the rise of Islam in Arabia, these countries were incorporated in a vast new empire stretching from the Atlantic and the Pyrenees in the West to the borders of China and India in the East. For a couple of centuries, this new empire was dominated by the Arabian conquerors, who formed a sort of conquistador aristocracy within it. The faith which they had brought, and the language in which its sacred scriptures were written, provided the basis and the medium of a rich new civilization, created by men of many faiths and nations, but expressed in the Arabic language and conforming to the standards of Islamic piety and aesthetics. In time, the Arabs were compelled to share or even relinquish their political primacy, giving place to new bureaucratic and military *élites* of alien origin. The Arabic language, however, retained its cultural pre-eminence long after its speakers had lost the realities of power. From the border of Persia and Iraq, right across the Fertile Crescent into North Africa, Arabic supplanted all previous official languages and remains the common language to the present day, with some local exceptions here and there.

East of the Perso-Iraqi border the Arab conquerors succeeded in imposing their religion, their script, and, for a while, their literary and scientific language, but not their speech or their national identity. The Persians were Islamized; they wrote Arabic, and indeed made an enormous contribution to the international literature of Islam written in the Arabic language. They remained Persian however, differing from the Arabs in speech and in sentiment. Like the other conquered peoples of the Arab Empire, they had an ancient language and literature; unlike them, they were sustained by still recent memories of independence and imperial greatness, and by a practical experience of administration and statecraft which soon won them a leading role in Arab government. During the ninth and tenth centuries Persia re-emerged on the political scene. Independent Persian dynasties appeared in what were formerly provinces of the Arab Empire, and a new Islamic Persian literary language developed with a rich and brilliant literature, responding to the tastes of Persian-speaking courts and patrons and reflecting the new self-awareness of the Persians as a distinct cultural group within Islam – in many ways the most advanced.

From about the tenth century onwards, Muslim Persian began to replace Arabic as the predominant literary medium outside the countries of Arabic speech. Arabic was no longer the

universal imperial and cultural language of Islam, as Latin had
been in medieval Europe. Instead, it was restricted, except for
religious and legal purposes, to these countries which, centuries
later, came to be called Arab. Farther east, not only in Persia
but also in the areas of Persian cultural influence in Turkey,
Central Asia, and India, Persian became the dominant literary
language, and the Persian replaced the Arabic classics as the
models for imitation. As the decline of the Arab lands coincided
with the renaissance of Iran, Cairo and Damascus and Baghdad
gave place to the cities of the Persians and Turks; these became
the great creative centres of Islamic civilization, now entering on
its second, and Persian, phase of achievement.

At about the same time, or slightly later, the third of the three
major peoples of the Islamic heartlands, the Turks, made their
appearance. They had come into the Middle East from Central
Asia, from their homelands beyond the Jaxartes (Sir Darya)
river. Most of the Turks had been pagans, though groups
among them had professed forms of Christianity, Manichaeism,
Judaism, and Buddhism. But in the course of time they were
almost without exception converted to Islam, and came to
play an important and then, for a long time, a dominant role
within the Islamic world.

The Turks at first came into the Middle East as soldiers and as
individuals, and soon predominated in the armies of Islam. In
the eleventh century they came as conquerors and colonists,
and set up a vast new empire in the heartlands of Islam, with
its centre in Persia. The first Arab Muslim conquerors had been
halted by the Byzantines at the Taurus mountains, which from
the seventh to the eleventh centuries marked the frontier
between Islam and Christendom. The Turks succeeded where
earlier invaders had failed, and pushed the barrier of Europe
further back, bringing Asia Minor into the world of Islam. After
the conquest they settled there in great numbers, so that
Western visitors – though not the inhabitants – began to call
the country Turkey, after the name of the dominant ethnic
and linguistic element there.

By conquest and settlement, Asia Minor became a predominantly Turkish land, linked by a continuous belt of Turkish
populations with the older Turkish lands in Central and Eastern
Asia. Almost everywhere else in the Middle East the Turks,

though a minority, formed the ruling element. Even in Persia, Syria and Egypt – even as far away as Muslim India, the ruling dynasties were Turkish, the armies were Turkish, though the overwhelming mass of the population were not. Through a millennium of Turkish hegemony it came to be generally accepted that Turks commanded while others obeyed, and a non-Turk in authority was regarded as an oddity. During this period, Turkish finally emerged as the third major language of the area. Like Persian before it, Turkish too was Islamized – written in the Arabic script, with a large Arabo-Persian vocabulary, representing the great heritage of Islamic – especially Perso-Islamic – civilization. This language provided the medium of the third great phase of Islamic Middle Eastern civilization – that of the Turks. Its first main centre was in the East, where a rich culture flourished in Herat, Samarkand and Bukhara in the eastern Turkish language. Thereafter it developed especially in the Ottoman Empire, the last and greatest of the Turkish Empires. By the sixteenth century Ottoman rule, suzerainty, or influence extended over almost all the lands of Arabic speech. Only in a few remote and inaccessible places – in faraway Morocco, in the mountain-valleys of Lebanon and the deserts of Arabia, did men of Arabic speech rule themselves. Their return to political independence, after an eclipse of nearly a millennium, has been one of the most explosive events of the twentieth century.

Islam, then, is the dominant faith, Arabic, Persian and Turkish are the dominant languages. The older religions and languages of the area have by no means entirely disappeared, and they survive in a mosaic of minorities that make the Middle East a museum of religious and linguistic history. At the time of the Arab conquests, Persia was Zoroastrian, the Fertile Crescent and Egypt Christian of various sects; both had important Jewish communities. Of these religions Zoroastrianism suffered most. The Persian state, unlike the Christian Empire, was completely overcome and destroyed. The Zoroastrians, lacking either the stimulation of powerful friends beyond the border enjoyed by the Christians, or the bitter skill in survival possessed by the Jews, fell into discouragement and decline. They took little or no part in the Iranian cultural and political revival in the Middle Ages, and are today represented only by a few thousand followers in Persia and a small community in the Indian sub-continent.

Christianity was defeated but not destroyed by the rise of Islam in the Middle East. The processes of settlement, conversion and assimilation gradually reduced the Christians from a majority to a minority of the population. They retained, however, a vigorous communal and religious life, and, secure in the tolerance of the Muslim state, were able to play a minor but significant role in the creation of classical Islamic civilization. The Crusades, with their legacy of fanaticism and suspicion, brought a permanent worsening in the relations of the Christians with their Muslim neighbours. Though still enjoying the basic rights secured by Muslim law, they were now socially isolated from the Muslims, and virtually excluded from the active cultural and political role they had played in the past. The first phases of westernization and national revival gave the Christian minority, for a while, a new and important function in Middle Eastern life and affairs. The shift from liberal patriotism to communal nationalism, and the growth of hostility to the Christian West, have again reduced it.

Only in one place do Christians as such still play a vital and decisive role. The republic of Lebanon in its present form is a new creation, but it expresses an old reality. The mountain has since medieval times been a refuge and a citadel of religious and political nonconformity; its people have an old tradition of initiative and independence. In an age of submission, the Lebanese amīrs succeeded, under both Mamluks and Ottomans, in preserving a considerable measure of autonomy. The Christian people of Lebanon, possessing both the Arabic language and a link with the West dating back to the Crusades, were able to make an immense contribution both to the spread of Western culture in the Middle East and to the emergence of a new Arab consciousness in response to it. Today, the role of the Lebanese in Arab affairs has been much reduced, and even that of the Christians inside Lebanon is no longer as great as it was. Even so, the city of Beirut remains one of the major commercial, financial, and intellectual centres of the Arab world.

The experience of the Jews in the Middle Ages was in general similar to that of the Christians, but diverged sharply in modern times. The Persian Empire had treated them well; the Byzan-

21

tines less well. The Arab conquest, which found important Jewish communities all over the Middle East, brought a general improvement in their status and security. The main centres of Judaic scholarship and culture had been in Persian Iraq and Byzantine Palestine. Under Muslim rule the Iraqi community flourished, while that of Palestine, now a minor and disturbed border province, fell into a decline. The Jews of Palestine had a particularly difficult time during the Crusades. They were massacred with the Muslims when the Crusaders captured Jerusalem in 1099; massacred again with the Christians when the Muslims finally reconquered Acre in 1291. Between these two extremes, however, they did manage to maintain some form of Jewish life in Palestine, and in the thirteenth century there were even waves of Jewish immigration both from Muslim North Africa and from Christian Europe, including a party of 300 French and English rabbis who arrived in Jerusalem in 1211. It was not, however, until after the Ottoman conquest at the beginning of the sixteenth century that fresh immigration from other Mediterranean lands led to the establishment of new and vigorous centres of Jewish intellectual activity in Jerusalem and Safed, with far-reaching influence among Jews in other countries, even in Christian Europe.

Like the Christians, the Jews also made an important though rather smaller contribution to classical Islamic civilization; like them, too, they suffered from the aftermath of the Crusades. The Ottoman conquests and the immigration of the relatively advanced Spanish and Portuguese Jews brought new opportunities, and during the fifteenth and sixteenth centuries they were able to acquire a position of some influence in the Ottoman lands. They lost it during the seventeenth century, and were eclipsed, during the eighteenth and nineteenth centuries, by the vigorous and rising eastern Christian communities.

Throughout the period of the dispersion Jews from other lands had from time to time settled in Palestine. Their numbers, however, had been small, and their purposes mainly religious. In the nineteenth century an entirely new type of immigrant began to come from Eastern and Central Europe, where the spread of nationalist ideologies provided a new ethos both for gentile persecution and for Jewish survival. The new immigrants – often called pioneers, settlers or colonists – were men whose faith was national rather than religious, and whose purpose in the Holy Land was not to pray and die but to work and live. The growth of militant anti-semitism in Europe gave new point and drive to Jewish nationalism. In 1914 there were about 85,000 Jews in Palestine; in 1948 they had increased to more than half a million, and were able to establish the State of Israel – the first Jewish state in Palestine (though not in other places) for 2,000 years. An incidental consequence was the virtual liquidation, by emigration, of the ancient Jewish communities in the Arab lands.

The rise of Jewish nationalism and the emergence of the Jewish State have been accompanied by the revival of Hebrew, which previously survived only as a language of religion, scholarship and literature, and as a medium of communication between learned Jews of different nationalities. In Israel it has become the national language, with Arabic as the second official language. Apart from a few isolated communities of Aramaic-speaking villagers, the other ancient languages of the Middle East have died out almost completely. In general, the Christian and Jewish minorities in the Arab lands speak Arabic, the Jews of Persia, Persian. The Greek- and Armenian-speaking Christians and Spanish-speaking Jews of Turkey constitute exceptions to the general pattern of linguistic assimilation.

Only one linguistic and ethnic minority of any importance has survived in the central lands of Middle Eastern Islam – the Kurds, who number several millions and live in parts of Turkey, Persia and Iraq. A deeply religious Muslim people, they have nevertheless retained their own language. Of late they have begun to show an increasing sense of national identity, and have subjected the dominant nations of the Middle East to the unnatural and unnerving experience of hearing, instead of making, nationalist claims and accusations.

On the fringes of the Middle East zone, a number of other languages remain in use. Afghanistan has two official languages, Pashto and Persian. In North Africa, the indigenous Berber languages are still spoken by very small groups in Libya and Tunisia, and by more important minorities in Algeria and Morocco. In all these areas Berber continues to lose ground to Arabic. In the Caucasian lands, a bewildering variety of languages still flourishes. Besides various Turkic and Iranian languages, they include Georgian, Armenian, Circassian, Chechen and Avar.

The three main languages of the Middle East show some variation in usage. Persian is the most unified and least extensive. It is the national language of Persia, with comparatively minor dialectal variation within the national frontiers. It is also used in parts of Afghanistan, and is very closely related to Tajik, which however is written in a different script. Pashto, Kurdish and some other minor languages belong to the Iranian family, but are distinct from Persian. Arabic, spoken over a vast area from Iraq to Morocco, shows a wide range of spoken dialects, some of them so far apart as to make conversation impossible. But the written language has remained the same, however, and its unifying power is being reinforced by the spread of education, the press, broadcasting, and the cinema. Turkish is the least unified of the three. At one time, despite a profusion of spoken dialects, the Turkic peoples had only two major literary languages, the Ottoman Turkish of Turkey, and the so-called Chagatay Turkish, which flourished in Central Asia. Both were written in the Arabic script, which, lacking vowels, tended to conceal dialectal variations, and made for a wider area of intelligibility. During the nineteenth century the Turkish of Azerbaijan also became the vehicle of a distinctive literary revival. It was however closely related to Ottoman Turkish, and much influenced by Ottoman literature. In the present century the Arabic script has been abolished in almost all Turkish-speaking areas. In Turkey it has been replaced by the Latin script; in the Soviet Union it was first replaced by the Latin script, and then, when the Turks had followed suit, by adaptations of the Russian Cyrillic. The unified Chagatay literary language has given way to a series of 'national' languages in the Soviet Middle East, based on spoken dialects and usually not mutually intelligible.

We have now defined the 'Middle East' in terms of geography and history, of religion, language and culture. It may be useful to attempt a closer definition, in terms of present-day political entities. Obviously, one cannot demarcate the frontiers of a zone or region, as one would of a state or province; except on the sea-coasts, the Middle East tapers off in an indeterminate borderland of countries that have much in common with it, yet are not wholly part of it. In current usage, the Middle East consists of Turkey, Persia, and perhaps Afghanistan; of Iraq and the Arabian peninsula; of the four Levant states of Syria, Lebanon, Israel and Jordan; and of Egypt, with variously defined extensions southwards and westwards into Arabic-speaking Africa. The northern limit of the Middle East is usually put at the Soviet frontier, but this is historically and geographically untenable. North of the frontier, in Transcaucasia, the Caucasus and Central Asia, are countries which until the nineteenth century were still an integral part of the Middle Eastern world. In earlier days, they had belonged to the great Arab, Persian and Turkic empires of Islam, of which such great Muslim cities as Samarkand and Bukhara were as essential a part as Baghdad or Cairo, Isfahan or Istanbul. Georgia and Armenia are Christian countries, on the edge of the Middle East; they have, however, at times been of some importance in Middle Eastern affairs, and many of their peoples have played a variety of roles in the Islamic lands. Other republics are inhabited by Turkic- or Iranian-speaking Muslims, closely akin in their religious, cultural and political traditions to the lands of what we now call the Middle East. It may be said that, apart from the remaining British footholds in southern Arabia, this is the only part of the Middle East that is still incorporated in a non-Middle Eastern political system.

It may seem that too much stress has been laid on Islam – on religion – in defining what is, after all, a twentieth century term. Religion means different things to different people. In the West it means principally a system of belief and worship, distinct from, and in modern times usually subordinate to, national and political allegiances. For Muslims it conveys a great deal more than that. Islam is a civilization – a term that corresponds to Christendom as well as Christianity in the West. No doubt, many local, national, and regional traditions and characteristics have survived among the Muslim peoples, and have gained greatly in importance in modern times; but upon all the peoples that have accepted them, the faith and law of Islam have impressed a stamp of common identity, which remains even when faith is lost and the law has been abandoned. In our own time that stamp is growing dim, but it is still by no means effaced.

This unity rested, in the first instance, on the Muslim creed that 'God is One and Muḥammad is His Prophet'; on the Qur'ān and the traditions; on the whole subtle and complex system of theology and law that was evolved from them. The teachings of historical Islam, besides moral and ritual precepts and theological dogmas, include much that in the West would be called law – civil, criminal, and even constitutional law. For the traditional, believing Muslim these laws emanate from the same source and possess the same authority as the laws of conduct and worship. The political traditions of the Islamic peoples were shaped for centuries by the formulations of the doctors of the holy law and by the memories of the Muslim empires of the past. Their languages, irrespective of origin, were written in the same Arabic script, and borrowed an immense vocabulary of Arabic words, especially of terms belonging to two closely related fields of endeavour – the one of religion and culture, the other of law and government.

It is not difficult to recognize an Islamic work of art. Anyone, even with a limited knowledge of art and architecture, can look through a folder of photographs of buildings and objects, and pick out those that are Islamic. The arcade and minaret of the mosque, the arabesque and geometrical patterns of decoration, the rules of sequence and association of both poetry and cookery – all these, despite many variations, show a fundamental unity of tradition and aesthetic which is Islamic, and which derives essentially from Middle Eastern – Arabic, Persian or Turkish – archetypes. In music, buildings, carpets and kebabs, this unity in diversity of Islamic civilization can be heard, touched, seen and tasted. It is also present, though less easy to identify and understand, in such things as law, government and institutions, in social and political attitudes and ideas.

The Islamic history of the Middle East was begun by the great Arab conquests of the seventh and eighth centuries, which, for the first time since Alexander, created a united imperial system from North Africa to the borders of India and China. The territorial and administrative unity of the Arab Empire was in time eroded and destroyed by invasion, dissension, and the processes of political fragmentation; the dominance of the Arab nation was challenged and ended by the rise of other nations within Islam. But the religious and cultural unity of

Middle Eastern Islam survived, and was symbolized in the ideal unity of the Caliphate, which all agreed to respect. There were moments of grave danger, when Islam was threatened from both east and west, but they were overcome. The Turks indeed came as conquerors – but they were converted and assimilated, and brought new strength and vigour to a dying society and polity. With that strength, Islam was able to hold and repel another invasion – that of the Crusaders, from the west.

From both directions, however, new and deadlier blows were to follow. On two occasions, the Islamic Middle East was crushed and overwhelmed by alien invaders who dominated it by force of arms, and, if they did not destroy the old civilization, sapped the confidence of those who maintained it and turned them on to new paths. The first was the invasion of the heathen Mongols from eastern Asia, who destroyed the Caliphate and, for the first time since the Prophet, subjected some of the heartlands of Islam to non-Islamic rule. The second was the impact of the modern West.

CHAPTER II

The Impact of the West

IT has been our practice for some time now to speak of the group of countries to which we belong as the West – a term which is no longer a purely geographical expression, but which also denotes a cultural, social, and latterly also a political and military entity. What are the geographical boundaries of this entity – not merely of the Western alliance, which are fairly obvious, but of the larger entity whose will to survive the alliance expresses? The westernmost limit of the West is clear enough; the Pacific coast – and dependencies – of North America. The eastern limit is more problematic. Leaving aside the local American concept of the West, which sometimes ends at the Rockies, the Mississippi, and, for New Yorkers, the Hudson, the West is generally understood to cover both shores of the North Atlantic, and to extend into Europe to a point which has been variously fixed, at various times and for various purposes, on the Channel, the Rhine, the Elbe, the Oder, the Vistula, the Bosphorus, and the Ural mountains, the conventional boundary between Europe and Asia.

The West is most easily defined in relation to the East – and of course there is more than one East. In the West, when we talk nowadays of East-West contrasts and conflicts, we usually mean the Cold War and its ramifications. In this sense, the East means the Soviet or Communist blocs (the two are no longer identical); the West means the Western alliance and its associates, sometimes humorously called the free world. It includes, in this context, a string of more or less dictatorial régimes on several continents, but excludes Sweden, Switzerland, Ireland and of course Finland.

The Soviet East is not however our only point of reference. There is also what one might call, with only apparent tautology,

28

the Oriental East – the many countries, societies and peoples of Asia, and for that matter of Africa who, however they may differ among themselves, have this much in common; that the white, Christian civilization of Europe and her daughters is alien to them, that they have for long been subject to its domination or influence, and that they are now bringing that subjection to an end. For many in the Middle East, as also, to a diminishing extent, in other parts of Asia, the real East-West struggle is this, and its purpose is to remove the last vestiges of Western Imperial domination in the East. The Western-Soviet conflict, according to this view, is an irrelevance – useful in many ways, no doubt, but not directly of concern to the oriental peoples. One might even argue that the Soviet Union itself is really a part of the West, with which it is linked by its dominant European population, its Judaeo-Christian and Greco-Roman background, its scientific and industrial development, and, some would add, its predatory habits. This view, however, does not yet command general support, and for most Easterners, the term West is still used in a narrower, more conventional sense.

In the Middle East the term West, expressing a cultural and political entity, is a comparatively new one – almost as new as the term Middle East, and like it of Western origin. But again, like the term Middle East, it denotes an ancient reality, for long known and familiar under other names. In recent years some attention has been given to the problem of national images and stereotypes, and some writers have sought to describe and classify the memories and prejudices that shape Western attitudes to the Middle East, and their influence on the formation of Western policy. Far less attention has been given to the origins and development of Middle Eastern attitudes towards the West, though these are of at least equal importance in the determining of relations between the two. In the absence of the rather Western habits of self-analysis and self-criticism, they may even be of greater importance.

The word West has been used since medieval times by Muslim writers – but not to denote Christian Europe. Islam had its own West, in North Africa and Spain, reaching as far as the Atlantic, and had no reason to apply this term to the infidel and barbarian lands that lay to the north of the Mediterranean

Sea. For the medieval Muslim, the world was divided into two great zones, the house of Islam and the house of war, with a perpetual state of war, or at best truce, between them. South and east of the house of Islam, the house of war was inhabited by pagans and idolaters, ready for conquest and ripe for conversion. North and north west lay the empires and kingdoms of Christendom, the greatest rival of the Islamic faith, the deadliest enemy of Islamic power. At first it was the Greek Christians of Byzantium who sustained the shocks of Islamic attack; later, while Byzantium faltered and finally succumbed to Turkish conquest, the Franks of Western Europe counter-attacked from Spain to Palestine, in Africa and in Asia. From late medieval times onwards the image of the European Christian has changed in Muslim minds. The Orthodox Greek, now a fellow subject of the Turkish Sultan, ceased to be a redoubtable foe and became a harmless neighbour. His place as enemy-in-chief was taken by the Frank. This term, commonly applied to the Crusaders in contemporary Arabic writings, was generalized to cover the Catholic – later also Protestant – peoples of central and western Europe, to distinguish them from the Muslims on the one hand, and the Greek Orthodox Christians on the other.

For the medieval Muslim the Franks were a race of barbarous infidels, of little interest or concern to the peoples of Islam. In the Muslim world view, Christianity, like Judaism, was in origin a true faith, representing an earlier link in the chain of divine revelations which had culminated in the final and perfect revelation vouchsafed to Muḥammad. What was true in it was preserved in Islam; the rest was accretion and distortion. Christianity, and with it the Christian civilization founded upon it, could accordingly be dismissed as something incomplete, superseded and debased. This view is certainly more tolerant than that of contemporary Christian Europe, which regarded Islam as something wholly false and evil, and it is reflected in the far greater tolerance accorded to the followers of the rival faith. This, however, did not make for any greater esteem. The Greeks were custodians of an ancient civilization, from whom something could be learnt, and with whom a form of coexistence had been evolved in the course of the centuries. The wild, fierce tribes of darkest Europe were thought to have no such redeeming features. It is noteworthy that while many works were translated into Arabic from Greek, Syriac, old Persian, and other languages, only one book – a late Roman history – was translated from Latin, and none from any other Western language throughout the Middle Ages.

This attitude may have been justified in the Dark Ages, when Frankish Europe was really backward and inferior; it can only have been reinforced by the conduct of the Crusaders in the Middle East and elsewhere. But already in the high Middle Ages it was becoming dangerously out of date.

From the end of the fifteenth century, the people of Europe embarked on a vast movement of expansion – commercial, political, cultural and demographic – which by the twentieth century had brought almost the whole world into the orbit of European civilization. It was an expansion at both ends; while the Portuguese and Spaniards, the English, Dutch and French sailed across the oceans from Western Europe to discover new worlds and conquer old ones, the Russians advanced southwards and eastwards across the steppes, towards the Middle East and into Asia. This process of expansion has gone through various forms and phases, and has been known by various names. One of them is colonization; others are the white man's burden, manifest destiny, and whatever synonym the Russians may use for the process that carried them from Muscovy to the Urals and from the Urals to the Pacific. In some areas the process of colonization was so successful and so complete that the previous inhabitants were displaced or reduced to insignificance, and the colonizers were strong enough to stand on their own feet without needing to lean any longer on the mother country. The French in North Africa did not quite reach this point; the English in North America did. In most of Asia and Africa the original cultures and peoples were too strong and too deeply rooted to be displaced, and the colonizers were limited to the role of overlords and rulers. The result was the classic colonial system of government, as it existed in the nineteenth and early twentieth centuries.

In the Middle East the impact of European imperialism was late, brief, and for the most part indirect. The impact of Europe was, however, profound and overwhelming.

At first it might well have seemed that the region was about to be caught between the two pincers of the Portuguese, advancing by sea from the south east, from their bases in India, and the Russians coming down from the north. But that danger was averted. A new power had arisen in the Middle East, able to hold both the Black and Red Seas for Islam, and to halt the northern and the southern intruders. The beginnings of European expansion had coincided with the emergence of two new Middle Eastern empires, the Safavid State in Persia, and the Ottoman State in Turkey. In the early years of the sixteenth century a bitter struggle between the two for supremacy in the Middle East resulted in an Ottoman victory. The Arab lands, already long accustomed to the rule of Turkish and other alien military castes, became part of the Ottoman Empire for 400 years.

Shielded by the military might of the Ottoman Empire from invasion and by the panoply of traditional learning from reality, the peoples of the Middle East continued to cherish the ancient human myth of self-sufficiency – to believe, as other societies before and after them have believed, in the immeasurable and immutable superiority of their own way of life, and to despise the barbarous Western infidel from an altitude of correct doctrine reinforced by military power.

The succession of Ottoman victories over Christian adversaries during the sixteenth century can only have encouraged this attitude; the military stalemate of the seventeenth century brought no real reason to modify it. The real change begins only when the Ottoman Empire suffered decisive and unmistakable defeats – defeats in battle, followed by loss of territory and peace treaties dictated by victorious enemies. It was a new and painful experience, and initiated a long and difficult adjustment, that is not yet completed.

The process began with the second Turkish siege of Vienna, in 1683. The Turkish failure this time was decisive and final, and was followed by a rapid advance of the Austrians and their allies deep into Ottoman territory. In 1696 the Russians seized Azov, thus gaining their first foothold on the Black Sea; in 1699 the Austrians imposed the treaty of Carlowitz – the first to be signed by the Ottoman Empire as a defeated power. Despite occasional rallies, the processes of defeat, humiliation and withdrawal continued during the eighteenth century, the bitterest blow of all being the Russian annexation, in 1783, of the old Turkish, Islamic land of the Crimea.

The problem first appeared as military, and the first remedies propounded were also military. The Ottoman armies had been defeated in the field by European armies; it might therefore be wise to adopt European weapons, training, and techniques. From time to time during the eighteenth century military instructors were imported from Europe, technical schools established, and Turkish officers and cadets instructed in the European arts of war. It was a small beginning, but an immensely significant one. For the first time young Muslims, instead of despising the uncouth Westernizers, were accepting them as guides and teachers, learning their languages, and reading their books. By the end of the eighteenth century the young artillery cadet who had learnt French to read his gunnery manual could find other reading matter, more explosive and more penetrating.

The military reforms, though the first and for long the most important, were not the only breaches in the wall of self-sufficiency. In 1729 the first Turkish printing press was established in Istanbul; by 1742, when it was closed, it had printed seventeen books, including a description of France by a Turkish ambassador sent there in 1721, and a treatise on the military arts as applied in the armies of Europe. The loss of cultural self-confidence can also be seen in the European influences that begin to affect Ottoman architecture, even religious architecture, as for example in the baroque ornamentation of the Nuruosmaniye mosque, completed in 1755.

The feeling of weakness and decline induced by military defeat must have been reinforced by the rapid increase in European exports to the Middle East, now extending beyond luxury products to include such staples as sugar and coffee. Both of these had once been exported from the Middle East to Europe; now they were brought, by European merchants, from the Americas to the markets of the Middle East. It was a time of discouragement, that variously found expression in a withdrawal of consent from Ottoman supremacy, in a first, tentative groping towards European ways – in the repetition of the old Islamic saying, with a new meaning and a new poignancy, that 'This world is the prison of the believers and the paradise of the unbelievers'.[2]

During the eighteenth century the chief territorial threat to the Middle East came from the north, where the military empire of Russia advanced steadily towards the Black Sea and the Caucasus. England and France – by now Asian as well as European powers – were the chief commercial rivals, competing in the markets of Egypt, the Levant and Persia.

The invasion of Egypt by a French expeditionary force under General Bonaparte in 1798 opened a new phase in the history of Western impact. Both Western and Middle Eastern historians have seen it as a watershed in history – the first armed inroad of the modern West into the Middle East, the first shock to Islamic complacency, the first impulse to westernization and reform. In all these respects it was to some extent anticipated by the Turkish defeats in the north, and by the Turkish response to them. Its importance, however, remains considerable. To the Muslims, Bonaparte demonstrated how easily a modern European army could invade, conquer and govern one of the heartlands of Islam; to the English, how easily a hostile power could cut their overland route to India. Both parties, in their different ways, learnt the lesson, drew inferences, and took action. The French expedition brought the problems of impact and response, in an acute form, to the Arab lands; it also inaugurated a century and a half of direct Anglo-French involvement in the affairs of these lands.

The menace from the north had by no means ended. By the eighteenth century the Russians had won control of the northern and eastern shores of the Black Sea, now no longer a Muslim lake. In 1800 they annexed Georgia; in 1806 they captured Baku, and in the early decades of the nineteenth century took from Persia and from local rulers the provinces now forming the Soviet republics of Armenia and Azerbaijan.

The eighteen fifties and sixties were a period of rapid and significant development in the Middle East. The Crimean War had the usual catalytic effect of a major war, bringing swift and sudden changes and a new intensity of feeling and experience. The alliance with Britain and France, and the arrival of British and French troops in Turkey, brought contacts with the West on a scale without precedent.

Halted in the nearer east by the Crimean War, the Russians turned their attention to Central Asia, where, in the eighteen sixties and seventies, they subjugated the Khanates of Khokand,

Bukhara and Khiva. The annexation of the area between the Caspian Sea and the Oxus river in the eighties consolidated their position in Central Asia and on the north-eastern frontier of Persia. A different kind of problem arose in Ottoman Europe, where the rise of nationalist movements threatened the Turks both with the loss of territory and the contamination of dangerous ideas.

In the Arab lands, the interference and influence of the West passed through several phases. In the first half of the nineteenth century, the Western interest was chiefly in trade and transit. True, there was some territorial encroachment, as in the Persian Gulf and in southern Arabia, where the British seized Aden in 1839, but these advances were limited to the far periphery, and concerned primarily with the security of the sea-lanes. The interests of Great Britain, by now the most active Western power in the Middle East, were served by the famous policy of 'maintaining the integrity and independence of the Ottoman Empire'. It seemed reasonable to assume that the Turks, as the dominant and established power in the area, would align themselves with those whose interests were purely economic and strategic, against a potential enemy whose aims were expansionist and disruptive. This British policy was abandoned only with extreme reluctance, and with many nostalgic hankerings. In a sense, first British and then American policies in the Middle East in recent years have represented a series of inconclusive attempts to discover or, failing that to create, a Middle Eastern power, whose integrity and independence they could maintain.

The second half of the nineteenth century brought important changes. The rapid modernization of the transit routes, the growth of direct Western economic and financial interest in the area, and, from the eighteen eighties onward, the extension of German influence in Turkey, led to a realignment of British policy. The occupation of Egypt, undertaken in 1882 for a limited purpose and a limited time, became permanent, and was extended to the Sudan. In 1918 the Ottoman Empire, which for four centuries had held the Arab lands, was defeated and destroyed, and a series of new, unfamiliar political structures was assembled from the debris.

Between 1918 and 1945 Britain and France, in fitful association and rivalry, were the dominant powers in the Arab East.

Aden, Palestine and the Sudan were ruled directly through régimes of a colonial type; elsewhere control – if that is the right word – was indirect. It was maintained through local governments, some of them under mandate, others nominally independent, with a variable and uncertain degree of responsibility for their own affairs. These arrangements ended in the years immediately following the second world war, when, with the exception of the last British footholds in Arabia, all the countries of the Arab Middle East acquired full political independence, and found new leaders and guides to exercise it on their behalf.

The century and a half of Anglo-French pre-eminence in the Middle East – from the mighty conflict of Nelson and Napoleon to the futile collaboration of Eden and Mollet – and the somewhat longer period of westernizing influences in Turkey, brought immense and irreversible changes, on every level of social existence. By no means all the changes were the work of Western rulers and overlords, most of whom tended to be cautiously conservative in their policies. Some of the most crucial changes were due to vigorous and ruthless Middle Eastern westernizers – rulers who sought to acquire and master the Western instruments of power, merchants anxious to make use of Western techniques for amassing wealth, men of letters and of action fascinated by the potency of Western knowledge and ideas. The processes of change are symbolically reflected in the progressive adoption of Western dress. Only once before in history had the Muslims departed from their own customs and adopted a foreign style of dress; that was when the Mamluk amīrs of late thirteenth-century Egypt, by order of the Sultan, wore Mongol robes and accoutrements and let their hair grow in the Mongol manner. The same kind of sympathetic magic no doubt inspired the adoption of trousers, tunics and frockcoats in the nineteenth century – first in the army, by order; then in the civil service, again by order; finally among the non-official urban literate classes, by a kind of social osmosis. The Mongol style was abandoned at the beginning of the fourteenth century, perhaps because the Mongols themselves were becoming Muslims; the coats and pants of Europe still remain, and have become the outward sign and symbol of literacy and modernity. In our own day the last bastion of Muslim conservatism is falling, as the turban and the tarbush disappear, and the brimmed, peaked and vizored headgear of the West replaces them.

The beginning was purely military – the simple desire for survival, in a world dominated by an expanding and advancing Europe. This required armies in the European style – a simple matter, so it seemed, of training and equipment, to be solved by borrowing a few instructors and indenting for the appropriate supplies. Yet the task of running the new style armies led inescapably to the building of schools to officer them – and the reform of education; to the formation of departments to maintain them – and the reform of government; to the creation and administration by the State of services and factories to supply them – and, very tardily, to the reform of the economy.

Economic and technological progress was for a long time largely the work of Europeans. It was they who built roads, railways, bridges, and ports, brought the steam engine in the nineteenth and the petrol engine in the twentieth century, gas and electricity, telegraphy and radio, and the first beginnings of industrial development. Sometimes they came in their own interest, as servants of their governments or of concessionary companies; sometimes as experts or advisers employed by Middle Eastern governments and other entrepreneurs. At first they employed only unskilled local labour, then also semi-skilled artisans; finally they were able to draw on important local reserves of technical and professional skill – of the men who ultimately took over from them.

With European weapons and technology came another importation, European ideas, which were to prove at least equally disruptive of the old social and political order. Until the eighteenth century, the world of Islam had been cut off from almost all intellectual and cultural contact with the West. The Renaissance and the new learning, the scientific, technological and intellectual movements of Christian Europe found no echo and awoke no response among peoples for whom they were profoundly alien and utterly irrelevant. Even the impact of European commerce and diplomacy, though it could not be wholly avoided, was cushioned and absorbed by an intermediate class of native Christians and Jews who, as merchants, agents, go-betweens and interpreters, protected their Muslim masters from the contamination of direct contact. The Ottoman Empire in the days of its greatness maintained no resident embassies abroad. Even its dealings with the foreign embassies in Istanbul passed through the hands of the Grand Dragoman, who was usually a Greek. There can have been very few Muslims with a reading knowledge of a Western language; with a few, trifling exceptions, there were no Arabic, Persian or Turkish translations of Western books. In the words of an Ottoman historian, 'Familiar association with heathens and infidels is forbidden to the people of Islam, and friendly and intimate intercourse between two parties that are to one another as darkness and light is far from desirable'.[3]

The military reform changed all that. Instead of an ignorant barbarian, the Frank became a teacher of the noblest and most crucial of arts – that of war. His language was no longer an 'uncouth jargon', as one writer had called it, but the key to essential knowledge.

The military reformers had intended to open a sluice gate in the wall, with a limited and regulated flow. Instead they admitted a flood – a foaming, frothing flood that came seeping and bursting through a thousand cracks, bringing destruction and the seeds of new life. It was a flood that seemed to have no end, as the apparently inexhaustible inventiveness of Europe produced more and newer ideas for each generation to master. During the nineteenth century two trends predominated, sometimes in harmony, often in conflict with one another – the radical liberalism of the French Revolution, and the authoritarian reformism of the Enlightenment.

There were many new channels through which Western ideas could percolate and penetrate to the hitherto sealed world of Islam. Such for example were the Muslim visitors from the Middle East, who now began to appear in increasing numbers in the capitals of Europe. Some few intrepid travellers had ventured, even in earlier times, to brave the dangers of unknown Europe, but from the Crusades to the seventeenth century barely a score have left any written record – almost all of them official envoys on special missions. In 1791 the Ottoman Sultan Selim III sent Ebubekir Ratib Efendi to Vienna, where he produced a detailed report on enlightened despotism at work, with recommendations for reform in the Ottoman Empire. In the succeeding years, the Sultan established the first resident embassies in London, Vienna, Berlin and Paris. They were followed by Persian embassies in the nineteenth century and, informally, by representatives of the new independent power that had arisen in Egypt under Muḥammad ʿAlī and his successors. At a time when a knowledge of foreign languages and an acquaintance with foreign countries were rare and vital qualifications, these embassies provided unique opportunities for acquiring them, and the men who had served in them formed an important element in the new political *élite*. Neither the *ulema** nor the army, but the translation chambers and the embassies were now the high road to influence and power.

After the diplomats, the second – and in the long run more important – group of Middle Easterners to appear in Europe were the students. The first Egyptian student mission was sent to Italy by Muḥammad ʿAlī Pasha in 1809, and by 1818 there were 23 Egyptian students in Europe. The first Persian student mission appeared in England at about the same time. In 1826 the Pasha of Egypt sent the first large Egyptian mission, of 44 students, to Paris. What the Pasha could do, the Sultan could do better, and in 1827 Sultan Mahmud II, despite strong religious opposition, sent a Turkish mission of about 150 students to various countries. In the course of the years hundreds of others followed them – the forerunners of the countless thousands that were still to come. It is a well known fact that students learn more from one another than from their teachers; and in the universities of Europe in the eighteen twenties, thirties, and forties there was much to learn.

It was no doubt in part because of this instruction that, during the eighteen sixties, a third group of visitors appeared – exiles. The Young Ottomans were a group of more or less liberal patriots who found it expedient to leave Turkey and continue their criticisms of the Sultan's ministers from Europe, where they published opposition journals in London, Paris, and Geneva, and had them smuggled into Turkey. They were followed in the later nineteenth century and early twentieth century by other liberal and patriotic groups, collectively and rather loosely known as the Young Turks. From time to time

* Arabic *'ulamā'* – professional men of religion.

other groups of political exiles came from the Middle East, but on the whole they have been surprisingly few and inactive.

Besides Middle Eastern visitors to the West, there were Western visitors to the Middle East – teachers and scholars, experts and advisers, missionaries and propagandists, as well as political and commercial entrepreneurs of many kinds. The first to exercise personal influence over young Muslims were the European military instructors, employed in Turkey, Egypt, and later Persia. Most of them were French, and the language they used was naturally French. The revolution in France did not break this link, and as late as 1796 the imperial Ottoman government sent a request to the Committee of Public Safety in Paris, to supply a number of military experts and technicians. They came – under the orders of the new French ambassador, General Aubert Dubayet, a native of New Orleans and a fervent revolutionary who had fought in America under Lafayette. The military school in Istanbul, we are told, had a library of 400 books, many of them French, including a set of the *Grande Encyclopédie*. Every university teacher knows that the presence of books in an academic library does not prove that anyone reads them – particularly when the books are in a foreign language, and express unfamiliar ideas. All we can say is that the books were accessible – and that some of the ideas appear in later generations. Muḥammad 'Alī in Egypt also recruited French officers, of whom many were available after 1815. His school of mathematics in Cairo also had a library with French books, including works of Rousseau and Voltaire, and books on European institutions. Many other military missions followed, from a variety of countries, among them a first group of American officers who went to Egypt after the Civil War. Of all groups in Middle Eastern society, the army officers have had the longest and most intensive exposure to Western influence, and have the most vital professional interest in modernization and reform. This may help to explain the Middle Eastern phenomenon, unusual in other parts of the world, of the professional officer as the spearhead of social change.

The officer-instructors were the first Western teachers; there were many others – teachers of every subject, in every kind of school. Some taught in the modern-style schools and colleges that were being set up, in increasing numbers, by Middle

Eastern governments; others in schools created by foreign missions and governments, as a service to humanity and an instrument of cultural policy. They were joined in both groups by growing numbers of westernized Middle Easterners, who had studied in Western schools at home or abroad, and mastered a Western language and skill.

The dissemination of Western knowledge and ideas was enormously helped by the spread, in various forms, of the European book. As a knowledge of European languages became commoner, European books found readers and, what is more important, translators. During the sixteenth century two books of Western origin are known to have appeared in Turkish; one was a history of France, translated in 1572 by order of the Reis Efendi, the Chief Secretary, in charge of foreign affairs; the other was an account of the discovery and wonders of the new world, compiled from European sources in about 1580. The seventeenth century brought a couple of books on history and geography and a treatise on the diagnosis and treatment of syphilis, which the Turks call *firengi*; the eighteenth added a few more, including some translations of French books on the military sciences, which were printed in Istanbul. Until the end of the eighteenth century there were still only a handful of Western works available in Turkish, most of them dry and factual compilations prepared for official use; there were none at all in Arabic or Persian.

The first impulse to the new translation movement seems to have come from the French, for frankly propagandist purposes. Thus, for example, the address of the National Convention to the French people, of October 9, 1794, was translated into Arabic and published in a quarto booklet with the French and Arabic texts on facing pages – a useful aid to students of language and of other things. Other French political writings were translated into Arabic and Turkish and distributed in the Middle East. The French expedition to Egypt made detailed arrangements for the publication of French news and opinion in Arabic.

The immediate impact of all this was, as far as we know, limited. Far more influential was the translation movement that developed during the nineteenth century in the three main centres – in Turkey, Egypt and Persia. At first it was all officially sponsored and reveals a rather official trend of thought. The first translations made and published under the auspices of Middle Eastern rulers include works on Napoleon and Catherine of Russia, Voltaire's *Peter the Great* and *Charles XII*, Robertson's *Charles V*, and the instructions of Frederick the Great to his commanders. Later the work was taken up and immensely developed by the enterprise of editors, publishers, printers and translators.

The West had offered new media of communication – printing in the eighteenth, journalism in the nineteenth, wireless and television in the twentieth century – all of which played a great role in the dissemination of Western and other ideas. The first newspapers were mainly official; the leading article in the first issue of the Ottoman official gazette, published on May 14, 1832, defines the function of the Press as to make known the true nature of events and the real purpose of the acts and commands of the government, in order to prevent misunderstanding and forestall uninformed criticism; a further purpose was to provide useful knowledge on commerce, science, and the arts. The first non-official newspaper in Turkish was a weekly founded in 1840 by an Englishman called William Churchill. It was followed by many others, in Turkish, Arabic, and Persian, as well as other languages.

With the Press came the journalist – a new and portentous figure in Middle Eastern life. Another newcomer, no less important, was the lawyer. In the old days, law was holy law, a branch of religious learning, and the only lawyers were the *ulema*. Legal and constitutional reform, the creation of modern laws and of courts to administer them, brought into existence a new class of secular advocates, who played a great role in the new political life, and in the application of new political ideas and methods.

The journalists and lawyers, like the new-style officers and officials, required a new type of education, in place of the traditional religious and literary learning of the past. Their pabulum was Western languages and literature, history, geography, and law, to which were later added economics and politics. Most of these subjects were new and strange; they were, however, familiar in that they were all literary in form, capable of being learnt from books or lectures, and then memorized.

They could thus be assimilated to traditional methods of education, relying chiefly on the authority of the teacher and the memory of the student.

The practical and physical sciences, however, were another matter. The once great Muslim tradition of scientific inquiry and experiment had long since atrophied and died, leaving a society strongly resistant to the scientific spirit. In the words of a Turkish historian of science, 'The scientific current broke against the dykes of literature and jurisprudence'.[4] No less serious an impediment was the deep-rooted social attitude to power, work and status that often makes the Muslim, even today, a bold and resourceful driver but a reluctant and unpredictable mechanic. Medicine, engineering, and other useful sciences were taught at the very first military schools; scientific treatises were among the first Western works translated into Turkish and Arabic – but many medical graduates preferred to become administrators rather than soil their hands with patients, and the scientific schools remained alien and exotic growths, in need of constant care and renewed graftings from the West. There has been no real development of original scientific work, such as exists in Japan, China or India, and each generation of students must draw again from the sources in the West, which has meanwhile itself been making immense progress. The result is that the disparity in scientific knowledge, technological capacity, and therefore of military power between the Middle East and the advanced countries of the West is greater now than a hundred and fifty years ago, when the whole process of westernization began.

From time to time in recent years Middle Eastern thinkers have put the question: what is the result of all this westernization? It is a question which we of the West may well ask ourselves too. It is our complacent habit in the Western world – the more so the further west one goes – to make ourselves the model of virtue and progress. To be like us is to be good; to be unlike us is to be bad. To become more like us is to improve; to become less like us is to deteriorate. It is not necessarily so. When civilizations clash, there is one that prevails, and one that is shattered. Idealists and ideologues may talk glibly of 'a marriage of the best elements' from both sides, but the usual result of such an encounter is a cohabitation of the worst.

The impact of the West in the Middle East has brought great benefits and will surely bring others – in wealth and comfort, knowledge and artefacts, and the opening of new ways that were previously shut. They are good roads, though it is not always certain where they lead.

Westernization – the work of westerners and still more of westernizers – has also brought changes of very doubtful merit. One of these is the political disintegration and fragmentation of the region. Until modern times there was an established political order in the Middle East, with the Shah as ruler of Persia and the Sultan as sovereign or suzerain of the rest. The Sultan may not always have been loved by his subjects, but he was respected and, what is more important, accepted, as the legitimate sovereign of the last of the Muslim universal empires. The Sultan was overthrown and the empire destroyed. In his place have come a succession of kings, presidents and dictators, who have managed for a time to win the acclamation and support of their peoples, but never that spontaneous and unquestioning acceptance of their right to rule, which the old legitimate sovereigns possessed, and which dispensed them from the need either for violent repression or for demagogic politics.

With the old legality and loyalty, the peoples of the Middle East also lost their ancient corporate identity. Instead of being members of a millennial Islamic imperial polity, they found themselves citizens of a string of dependencies and then nation-states – most of them entities new to history, and only now beginning to strike roots in the consciousness and loyalties of their peoples.

The undermining and collapse of the old political order was accompanied by a parallel process of social and cultural disintegration. The old order may have been decayed, but it was still functioning, with a mutually understood system of loyalties and responsibilities binding the different groups and classes of society together. The old patterns were destroyed, the old values derided and abandoned; in their place a new set of institutions, laws, and standards were imported from the West, which for long remained alien and irrelevant to the needs, feelings, and aspirations of the Muslim peoples of the Middle East. It may well be that these changes were 'necessary' and 'inevitable', as these words are used by historians. The fact remains that they brought a period of formlessness and irresponsibility deeply damaging to Middle Eastern polity and society.

The economic consequences of westernization arc too well known to need more than a brief mention – the explosive rise in population, above all in Egypt, unaccompanied by any corresponding increase in food supply; the widening and more visible gap between rich and poor; the creation of new appetites and ambitions, more rapidly than the means of satisfying them. These tensions have been building up for some time past. In our day they have come to breaking point.

The attitude of the peoples of the Middle East towards the West has gone through several phases. For many centuries, while Europe was rising to greater and greater heights of achievement, the East sank in the comfortable torpor of decay, unwilling and unable to perceive or to understand the vast changes that were taking place. In the nineteenth century their illusions of superiority and self-sufficiency were finally shattered, and they awoke to a disagreeable reality in which their countries, their resources, their civilizations, their very souls were menaced by a Europe which was rich and powerful beyond belief, and which, in its limitless self-confidence, aggressiveness and acquisitiveness, seemed to be bringing the whole world within its grasp.

In this situation, the mood of the Easterner began to change from ignorant complacency to anxious emulation. The West was great and strong; by study and imitation, it might be possible to discover and apply the elusive secret of its greatness and strength, and generations of eager students and reformers toiled in the search. They may not have loved us, or even understood us, but they did admire and respect us. Today they usually do neither.

The mood of admiration and imitation has given way to one of envious rancour. This change has no doubt been helped by our own lamentable political and moral failures; it has also been helped by the lessons of liberty and human self-respect which we of the West have taught. In the words of Muḥammad Iqbāl, in a poem addressed to England, on the desire of the Easterner for freedom –

It was the scent of the rose that drew the
    nightingale to the garden:
Otherwise the nightingale would not even have
    known that there was a garden.[5]

But most of all the present wave of hostility is due to the crisis of
a civilization, reacting at last against the impact of alien forces
that have dominated, dislocated, and transformed it. It is some
of the processes of impact, response, and reaction that must
now claim our attention.

CHAPTER III

The Quest for Freedom

IN 1878 a young Turkish diplomat called Sadullah went to see the Great Exhibition in Paris. In a letter describing what he saw he wrote: 'In front of the central gate there is a statue of freedom; she has a staff in her hand and is seated on a chair. Her style and appearance convey this message: "Oh worthy visitors! When you look upon this fascinating display of human progress, do not forget that all these achievements are the work of freedom. It is under the protection of freedom that peoples and nations attain happiness. Without freedom, there can be no security; without security, no endeavour; without endeavour, no prosperity; without prosperity, no happiness ..." '6

Liberty, in other words, is an essential prerequisite to the pursuit of happiness, through the intermediate stages as indicated.

In these words Sadullah was expressing a view common among Middle Eastern explorers of Europe in the nineteenth century – the view that political freedom was the secret source of Western power and success, the Aladdin's lamp with which the East might conjure up the genie of progress and win the fabulous treasures of the gorgeous and mysterious Occident.

At this point some definition of terms is necessary. Freedom and independence are often loosely used as synonyms, but should be differentiated. For the sake of clarity, we may for the moment define freedom as a political term referring to the position of the individual within the group – to the immunity of the citizen from arbitrary and illegal action by the government, and to his right to participate in the formation and conduct of government. Independence on the other hand refers to the position of the group in relation to other groups – to the formation and sovereignty of the state, untrammelled by any superior,

47

alien authority. Freedom and independence are thus quite different – sometimes even mutually exclusive – things, and represent different objectives. Freedom is maintained and exercised through a form of political organization which is, by those who practise it, now usually called democracy. It is true that in modern times the word democracy has been used with many adjectives and in many other senses – social, organic, basic, guided and popular; the neo-marxist dictatorship of the secretariat; the unanimous plebiscitary ratification of military *res gestae*; royal affability and party public relations. Our present concern is with none of these, but with free, representative and constitutional government, and with the attempt to introduce such government in the Middle East. It is a sad story.

The idea of political freedom first appeared in the Middle East at the end of the eighteenth century, grew and developed during the nineteenth, and in most of the area died out in the middle of the twentieth.

Despite the elective doctrines of the Muslim jurists, enshrining the memories of a remote nomadic past, the political experience of the Middle East under the caliphs and sultans was one of almost unrelieved autocracy, in which obedience to the sovereign was a religious as well as a political obligation, and disobedience a sin as well as a crime. Though the Muslim sovereign was an autocrat, he was not a pure despot. He was always subject, in theory and to a large extent even in practice, to the Holy Law of Islam; by the eighteenth century the effective authority of the Ottoman Sultan was limited by such entrenched and powerful groups as the *ulema*, the janissaries, and the provincial notables. There were, however, no corporate, established bodies to represent them. Islamic law knows no corporate legal persons; Islamic history shows no councils or communes, no synods or parliaments, nor any other kind of elective or representative assembly. It is interesting that the jurists never accepted the principle of majority decision – there was no point, since the need for a procedure of corporate, collective decision never arose. In heaven there was one God, and one alone; on earth there was no court but a single judge, no state but a single ruler.

This ancient tradition of autocracy and acquiescence was first breached by the impact of the ideas of the French Revolution. Interest was soon aroused. In April 1797 the English traveller W. G. Browne had a conversation with Ḥasan Junblāṭ, a Druze chief in Kasrawan, in the north Lebanon: 'He was very inquisitive as to the motives and history of the French Revolution, and the present religious creed of that nation; on hearing the detail on which, he however made no interesting remarks'.[7] In the following year, with the arrival of the French in Egypt, fuller and perhaps more stimulating details were available. In Turkey the ideas of the revolution became known even earlier, and were actively propagated by the French embassy and its friends. On July 14, 1793 the French community had a solemn celebration, at which they read the Declaration of the Rights of Man, swore allegiance to the Republic, and drank the health of the French Republic and Selim III, of the soldiers of the motherland and the friends of liberty, and of universal brotherhood. The inauguration of the republican flag the following year provided the occasion for a still bigger celebration, culminating in a salute from two French ships moored off Seraglio Point. The party ended with the guests dancing a republican *carmagnole* around the tree of liberty which had been planted in the soil of Turkey, in the grounds of the French embassy.

There is no evidence that the Turks were much interested in these proceedings. But the ideas which they represented began to percolate, at first in a very limited circle, then to larger and larger groups among the intellectual *élite*. The tree of liberty bore fruit. The French Revolution was the first great movement of ideas in Europe that was not expressed in more or less Christian terms, and its doctrines could therefore spread, unhampered, through the new channels that were being opened into the world of Islam. A new generation was to grow up, fascinated by the ideals of liberty, equality, and fraternity. It was some time before their successors decided that the first two were mutually exclusive, and the third in need of redefinition.

The first step in the direction of constitutional government was taken as early as 1808, when the Grand Vizier Bayrakdar Mustafa Pasha convened an assembly of dignitaries and provincial lords and notables in Istanbul; after some negotiations, they signed – and made the Sultan sign – a deed of agreement.

Various interpretations have been placed on these events, which in any case came to nothing. *Ad hoc* consultative meetings, called *mashwara*, were not uncommon in the Ottoman Empire. What was new, and important, was that the 'deed of agreement' was a reciprocal contract, negotiated between the Sultan and groups of his servants and subjects, in which the latter appear as independent contracting parties, receiving as well as conceding certain rights and privileges.

Consultation is recommended in the Qur'ān, and was practised from time to time by sovereigns with their counsellors, officials, and courtiers. The nineteenth century brought the first attempts to extend and to institutionalize it. The French had set an example by appointing several consultative bodies during their occupation of Egypt. In 1829 Muḥammad 'Alī Pasha set up a council of consultation (*majlis mashwara*) of 156 members, all nominated. They consisted of 33 high officials of the central government, 24 provincial officials, and 99 notables. They met only once a year, for a day or longer if necessary, and discussed such topics as agriculture, education and taxes. When Muḥammad 'Alī occupied Palestine and Syria, his governors appointed a consultative council of notables (*majlis shūrā*) in each of the main towns, with advisory and some judicial functions. In 1845 the Ottoman Sultan Abdülmejid also experimented with an assembly of provincial representatives. Two were to be chosen from each province, 'from among those who are respected and trusted, are people of intelligence and knowledge, who know the requisites of prosperity and the characteristics of the population'.[8] Despite these high qualifications the experiment produced no results and was abandoned. A similar and equally inconclusive experiment was held in Persia shortly after.

While Sultans and Pashas experimented with nominated advisory bodies, some of their subjects began to play with more radical ideas. In classical Islamic usage *ḥurriyya*, freedom, was primarily a legal term, denoting the legal status of the free man, as opposed to that of the slave. The first references to political freedom in Muslim writings are hostile and suspicious; it is something foolish and evil, much the same as libertinism and anarchy. But soon a more positive attitude appears. In the eighteen twenties and thirties young Muslims began to come to Europe, in search of enlightenment and of the elusive secret of Western power. In the Europe of that time there was no lack of voices to commend the merits of liberalism, the cause of idealists and businessmen alike–and what, to the alien visitor, could have seemed more extraordinary, more distinctive of the West than constitutional and representative government? It is not surprising that many of them decided that this was the talisman they sought.

One of the first Middle Easterners to argue the merits of parliamentary government was an Egyptian, the Azhari Shaykh Rifāʿa Rāfiʿ al-Ṭahṭāwī. In 1826, at the age of twenty-five, he accompanied the Egyptian student mission to Paris, and stayed there until 1831. He was not himself a member of the mission, but was their religious preceptor. He seems, however, to have learnt more than any of his wards. His book, containing an account of what he saw in France, was published in Arabic in 1834, and in a Turkish translation in 1839. It contains a description of parliamentary government, the purpose of which is to secure government under law, and to protect the subjects from tyranny – or rather, as he observes, to give the subjects the opportunity to protect themselves. Shaykh Rifāʿa witnessed and explained the 1830 revolution in which, he says, the king was removed for violating the constitution and attempting to curtail the freedoms which it assured. He attached great importance to the Press, 'the sheets called newspapers (*al-waraqāt .. al-musammāt biʾl-jurnālāt waʾl-gāzeṭāt*)'[9] as a safeguard against misrule and a medium for the communication of knowledge and ideas. The book includes a complete translation of the French constitution, with comments.

Shaykh Rifāʿa was no liberal revolutionary, but a loyal servant of Muḥammad ʿAlī and his successors, whom he served with distinction for many years. His political teachings, after his return to Egypt, tended to be cautious and conservative; the sovereign must rule as well as reign, but should use his power wisely and justly, with proper respect for the law and for the rights of the subject – a position closer to the enlightened despots than to the Revolution. Such exhortations to the sovereign to govern with justice were in the classical tradition of Islamic political writings; what is new is the idea that the subject has a *right* to justice, and that some sort of apparatus might be set up to secure that right. The same kind of modified conservatism can be found in an essay written by Sadik Rifat Pasha, the Turkish ambassador in Vienna in 1837, perhaps under the influence of Metternich. He too speaks of the 'rights of the people' and 'the rights of freedom', by which he meant freedom from oppressive and arbitrary government.[10]

But in fact government was becoming more and not less oppressive. The creation of a modern administrative apparatus on the one hand, and the introduction of modern methods of communication and coercion on the other, were tightening the screws of government; the old intermediate limiting powers of the religious, military and landowning interests were abrogated or enfeebled, leaving the state with nothing but its own edicts and charters to restrain it. Little understood by the people, half-heartedly applied by the officials, supported by no strong body of either interest or opinion, these charters of civil rights, however well-intentioned, could have but little effect.

At this point a cleavage begins to appear between reformers and radicals – the Ottoman heirs of the Enlightenment and of the Revolution. The former, usually conservative and authoritarian in politics, seek to modernize in order to strengthen and enrich their countries, and use all the powers of the reinforced state for this purpose. The latter, including both reactionary and progressive elements, criticize the reforms and still more the manner of their application, and seek a remedy in constitutionalism, in ideas which they derive from European liberalism but often attribute to Qur'anic and other Islamic doctrines. These ideological differences are complicated – sometimes even motivated – by personal and political quarrels, and notably by the rivalry between Ottoman Istanbul and Khedivial Cairo which, throughout the nineteenth and early twentieth centuries, was an important element in Middle Eastern political life.

In the sixties and seventies of the nineteenth century constitutionalism in the Middle East seemed to be taking important steps forward. In 1861 the Bey of Tunis, then an autonomous monarchy under a loose Ottoman suzerainty, proclaimed a constitution – the first in any Islamic country. The Bey remained head of the state and of the faith, and retained executive power for himself and his ministers, with whom, however, he was responsible to a Grand Council of 60 members, some appointed by the Bey and some co-opted, for a term of five years. The judicial power was to be exercised by an independent judiciary, the legislative power shared by the Council with the Government. The Tunisian constitution was suspended in 1864, but the trend continued elsewhere. The year 1866 brought important developments in other lands under Ottoman suzerainty, nearer home. In Roumania a liberal constitution was proclaimed, based on the Belgian constitution of 1831; in Egypt the Khedive Ismāʿīl created a Consultative Assembly of Delegates (*majlis shūrā al-nuwwāb*), consisting of 75 delegates elected for a three-year term by a system of indirect, collegiate elections. The Young Ottoman constitutionalists who in 1867 sought refuge in England and France received financial support from the Khedive's brother, Mustafa Fazil Pasha, and then from the Khedive Ismāʿīl himself. After some setbacks their cause seemed to triumph, when in 1876 an Ottoman constitution was promulgated in Istanbul by the new Sultan, Abdül-hamid II. This too was influenced by the liberal monarchical Belgian constitution, both directly and through the Prussian constitutional enactment of 1850, in which Belgian liberal principles were adapted in a number of respects to the more authoritarian traditions of Prussia. It provided for a parliament, consisting of a nominated senate and an elected chamber, with some, rather perfunctory, recognition of the principle of the separation of powers.

The effective life of the constitution was brief. After a general election, the first Ottoman parliament assembled in March 1877, and sat until June. New elections were then held, and a second parliament met in December. It soon began to show alarming vigour, and on February 14 was summarily dismissed by the Sultan. The first Ottoman parliament had sat for two sessions, of about five months in all; it did not meet again for thirty years.

These early constitutional reforms were not only gestures of emulation towards Europe; they also had a quality of propitiation. They were intended to prove that their authors were also civilized and progressive by European standards, and therefore worthy of respect – to qualify for loans and other forms of favourable consideration, and, in extreme cases, to ward off

interference and occupation. In these purposes they secured only
fitful and limited success. Neither the short-lived Tunisian
constitution nor the slightly longer Egyptian parliamentary
experiment did anything to halt the downward plunge to
bankruptcy, disorder, control and occupation. Some observers
thought they might even have helped it. In Turkey Sultan
Abdülhamid, the last of the great authoritarian reformers of
the nineteenth century, decided to dispense with the trappings
of democracy, and to achieve modernization by more traditional
methods.

For the next thirty years the only place in the Middle East
where parliamentary institutions of any kind existed was
Egypt. The assembly of 1866 held its prescribed three terms,
and was succeeded by further, similar assemblies, elected in
1869, 1876, and 1881. In 1882, during the 'Urābī revolt, the
assembly prepared and promulgated a draft parliamentary
constitution. The draft was abrogated and the assembly dismissed when 'Urābī failed. A new start was made after the
British occupation of 1882, when Lord Dufferin, who was sent
to Egypt to reorganize the government of the country, wrote to
the Foreign Secretary, Lord Granville, in London that the
British occupation should be based on 'national independence
and constitutional government'.[11] The first objective, because of
changing circumstances, received less attention than it required,
though more than is sometimes allowed. The second was a
matter of continuing concern to the British authorities, in both
London and Cairo, who made a serious attempt to place the
government of the country on a constitutional basis and allowed
the Press a measure of freedom which, though limited, was
sufficient to attract creative and critical writers from neighbouring territories enjoying full independence but no freedom. The
new Organic Law for Egypt, promulgated in May 1883, provided for two quasi-parliamentary bodies; the first was a legislative council of 30 members, 14 nominated and permanent,
16 indirectly elected for six years; the second, the General
Assembly, consisted of the Khedive's ministers, the members of
the legislative council, and 46 others elected for six years. These
bodies, with their restricted and apathetic electorates, their
limited and advisory powers, their brief and infrequent meetings, must have seemed a poor substitute for the constitutional

aspirations of the liberals. They functioned, however, regularly and not altogether ineffectively, from 1883 to 1912, and were able on more than one occasion to take an independent line, asserting their views and rights against the Khedive and sometimes against the occupying power. Their growing authority was recognized in 1913, when they were merged together in a new and rather more powerful body, called the Legislative Assembly. This consisted of the ministers, 17 nominated and 66 elected members, indirectly elected for a term of six years, one third every two years. This rule of rotation was perhaps due to American influence. The first-degree elections were in October 1913; the first session lasted from January to June 1914. There were no more elections or assemblies until after the war.

Meanwhile far more radical developments had been taking place further north. In 1905 a thrill of exultation passed through Asia when for the first time an Asian power, Japan, was able to defeat a European great power, Russia, in battle on both land and sea. There were some who made the further observation that the oriental victor was the only Asian country that had adopted a form of parliamentary and constitutional government, while the European loser was the only European power that had refused to do so. In Russia, the Tsar himself, faced with revolution, seemed to concede the point, by granting a form of constitution and convening the first Duma. In Egypt the nationalist leader Muṣṭafā Kāmil wrote a book called *The Rising Sun*, showing by the example of Japan how an oriental nation could achieve self-renewal and success; in Turkey two officers wrote a five-volume illustrated history of the Russo-Japanese war; in Persia, in the summer of 1906, a constitutional revolution forced the Shah to convene a national assembly which drafted a liberal constitution. Two years later the Young Turk revolutionary officers, fearing – mistakenly as it turned out – that the meeting of the English and Russian sovereigns at Reval portended the demise of the Sick Man of Europe, decided on an immediate dose of the constitutional elixir, and forced the reluctant Sultan to restore the constitution of 1876, thus inaugurating the second, somewhat longer, and far stormier interlude of constitutional government in Turkey.

The victory of the allied and associated powers over their

somewhat less democratic opponents in 1918, with the collapse of the only autocracy in the allied camp, seemed to provide final proof of the proposition that democracy makes a state healthy, wealthy and strong. In Damascus, Prince Fayṣal's Syrian Congress drafted a constitution for a limited, parliamentary monarchy. It was abandoned with the arrival of the French on July 19, 1920. The British and French, as mandatory powers, created constitutional republics and monarchies in their own image, in the countries under their control; elsewhere too, in the years following the victory, constitutions and parliaments spread all over the Middle East in what seemed a universal triumph of liberal and democratic principles.

Today this great experiment must be written off as an almost complete failure. The oldest surviving constitutional régime in the Middle East at the present time is that of Persia, where the constitution promulgated after the liberal revolution of 1906 remains in force, though barely in effect. The second oldest is that of Lebanon, where the 1926 constitution, despite some vicissitudes and fairly drastic emendations, has been retained. Elsewhere, all the constitutions adopted in the democratic millennium of the nineteen twenties have been abandoned or replaced, by more or less violent processes. In Turkey, the will and the desire remain. The military junta which destroyed the old régime in 1960 itself withdrew, with unique self-effacement, to allow the emergence of a new constitutional democracy. The government of the second Turkish republic is so determined to prove that democracy can work in Turkey that it is a criminal offence punishable by a term of imprisonment to say that it cannot. In Egypt, which has the longest and, on the whole, the most successful record of parliamentary government in the Arab world, the abandonment of the Western form of representative, liberal democracy was most final and most complete. Elsewhere the captains and the kings divide the Arab lands, and neither show any inclination to depart.

There are only three countries in the Middle East today where political democracy functions at all – in Israel, Lebanon and Turkey. They are also the three most European states in the area – the first non-Islamic, the second only half-Islamic, the third wholly Islamic, but transformed by two secularist revolutions. This has led some observers to conclude that Islam

and democracy are incompatible – that is to say, that there is
something in the Islamic pattern of social and political behaviour that impedes or prevents the proper working of parliamentary institutions. In support of this thesis, they point to the
mishaps and breakdowns of parliamentary government in the
Islamic states, old and new, where it has been tried – including
even Pakistan, where its collapse is in striking contrast with the
vigorous democracy of India, another successor state of the same
imperial régime.

'Semites', says T. E. Lawrence, 'have no half-tones in their
register of vision ... they exclude compromise, and pursue the
logic of their ideas to its absurd ends ...'[12] That there is something in this, no observer of Middle Eastern affairs can deny.
But those who go on to argue that Arabs and other Muslims
are necessarily incapable of democratic government are surely
guilty of the same kind of absurdity. Some features of traditional Islamic civilization are distinctly favourable to democratic development – such as tolerance, social mobility, and
respect for law. Classical Islam succeeded, as Christendom
never really succeeded, in combining religious tolerance with
deep religious faith, extending it not only to unbelievers but
also – a far more exacting test – to heretics. The coexistence of
differing schools of holy law, all regarded as orthodox, is
another example of Islamic tolerance and compromise.
Socially, Islam has always been democratic, or rather equali-
tarian, rejecting both the caste system of India and the aristocratic privilege of Europe. It needed no revolution to introduce the 'career open to the talents' to the Islamic world; it
was there from the start, and, despite the inevitable tendency to
the formation of aristocracies, it was never really eliminated.
Islamic theory has always insisted on the supremacy of the law,
and the subordination to it of the sovereign. In the Ottoman
Empire the hierarchy of the *ulema* achieved considerable
success in enforcing this principle. There remains of course the
political difficulty – the total absence, despite the elective
doctrine of the jurists, of any conception or experience of
representative or limited government of any kind. It is this no
doubt that underlies the theory that democracy cannot work in
Islamic lands. That there is a predisposition to autocratic
government among Muslim peoples is clear enough; that there

is an inherent incapacity for any other has yet to be proved.

There is always something disquieting about a hypothesis that presumes a kind of political original sin in human societies; this one is in any case unnecessary, for there is enough in the recent history of the Middle East to explain the failure of constitutional democracy, without recourse to political theology. It is easy and tempting for us in the West to adopt an attitude of superiority, contemptuous or tolerant, and to ascribe the breakdown of our distinctive institutions, among other peoples, to the lack on their part of some of our distinctive virtues. It is easy, but it is not wise, and certainly not helpful. We of the West no doubt all share the belief that liberal democracy, with all its weaknesses, is the best instrument that any section of the human race has yet devised for the conduct of its political affairs. At the same time we should remain aware of its local origin and character, and try to avoid the primitive arrogance of making our own way of life the universal standard of political morality. 'He is a barbarian', says Caesar of Britannus in Shaw's play, 'and thinks that the customs of his tribe and island are the laws of nature'. Political democracy is a good custom. It has already spread far from its native land, and in time will surely spread much farther. It is not however a law of nature, and in some areas has been tried, found wanting, and abandoned. We must ask why.

In the Middle East a serious attempt was made to introduce and to operate liberal democracy, with written constitutions, elected, sovereign parliaments, judicial safeguards, a multitude of parties, and a free Press. With few and atypical exceptions, these experiments have failed; in some countries democratic institutions are in a state of disrepair or collapse; in others they have already been abandoned, and the search begun for other paths to the pursuit of happiness.

Today, with the hindsight of history to guide us, we can see many of the causes clearly enough. A political system taken over ready-made not merely from another country but from another civilization, imposed by Western or westernized rulers from above and from without, could not respond adequately to the strains and stresses of Islamic, Middle Eastern society. Democracy was installed by autocratic decree; parliament sat in the capital, operated and supported by a minute minority, whose happy immersion in the new game of parties, programmes and politicians was ignored, or else watched with baffled incomprehension, by the great mass of the people. The result was a political order unrelated to the past or present of the country, and profoundly irrelevant to the needs of its future. The parliament at Westminster is the result of centuries of history, with its roots in the Anglo-Saxon *witenagemot*; it is the apex of a pyramid of self-governing institutions, with its base at the parish pump. It was evolved by Englishmen, on the basis of English experience, to meet English needs. The parliament of Cairo was imported in a box, assembled and ready for use, without even a set of do-it-yourself instructions. It responded to no need or demand of the Egyptian people; it enjoyed the backing of no powerful interest or body of opinion.

When a piece of expensive imported machinery falls apart in our hands, we are apt to lay the blame, not on our own inexpert handling, but on the manufacturers and suppliers. The West, which acted in both capacities, has had perhaps more than its fair share of blame for the breakdown of democracy. It cannot, however, wholly disclaim responsibility. One fault was the failure adequately to support those who were its most enthusiastic disciples. Another lies in the mandatory system, which was supposed to provide a training in responsibility, but instead gave an advanced training in irresponsibility. The position was if anything rather worse in those countries that remained nominally independent, but subject to constant interference. There is a case to be made for as well as against the imperial peace – Persian, Roman, Arab, Turkish, French or British – as a stage in the development and spread of civilizations; there is little that can be said in defence of the so-called imperialism encountered by the Middle East in the first half of the twentieth century – an imperialism of interference without responsibility, which would neither create nor permit stable and orderly government. Perhaps one of the most significant distinctions in the ex-imperial countries of Asia and Africa is between those that were directly administered through a colonial or imperial civil service, and those that were under some form of indirect rule or influence. The people of the latter group of countries got the worst of both worlds, receiving neither the training in administration of the colonial territories, nor the practice in responsibility of the old independent states. The system of direct rule, apart from the useful legacy of an efficient modern bureaucracy, often has the additional merit of clarity. In British India, for example, the transfer of power and responsibility was clear, precise, and unequivocal. Until August 15, 1947 the British were responsible; thereafter the British ceased to be and the Indians became responsible, and no serious observer has claimed or suspected otherwise. In Egypt, it would be difficult to agree on the date of the effective transfer of responsibility within half a century. This situation, with its parallels in other Middle Eastern countries, produced a generation of politicians more apt to demand responsibility than to accept it, with a tendency to take refuge from reality that has not entirely died out. Even today, there are still politicians who reiterate the by now pointless demand that we treat them as responsible adults and equals – but show by their words and deeds that they count on us not to do so. There are too many who are willing to profit from that most insidious form of Western prejudice which shows itself by expecting and accepting a lower standard of behaviour and performance.

There is of course more to the question of democratic viability than cultural traditions and political aptitudes. Israel and Lebanon, two of the exceptions to the record of failure, are not only culturally westernized; they are also relatively well-fed, well-clothed, and well-housed. A small and highly urbanized population in a small area, with good communications and a high standard of education and of living, gives democracy a rather better chance than the sprawling impoverished peasant slums that make up a good deal of the rest of the Middle East. After Israel and Lebanon, Turkey has the highest *per capita* income, the greatest mileage of railway in relation to area, the highest rate of literacy in the Middle East – though, as against this, Egypt has more industry, more town-dwellers, and has, or until recently had, more newspaper readers. There would seem to be some correlation between democracy and material progress, though which is the chicken and which is the egg is another question.

This much can be said with reasonable certainty – that many of the social and economic factors that helped to make democracy work in other parts of the world are missing in the Middle

East, or at least were missing in the crucial period when the experiment was tried. Society was still composed mainly of landlords and peasants. The commercial and industrial middle class, such as it was, consisted largely of foreigners and of members of minorities, who as such were unable to play the classical political and cultural role of the bourgeoisie in Western societies; the new, Muslim professional class of lawyers, journalists and teachers lacked the economic power and cohesive force to play any really independent role. The industrial working class barely existed; the peasant masses and urban *lumpenproletariat* were poor, ignorant and unorganized, still totally unfitted for participation in political life. In such a society no new and greater loyalty could arise to transcend the old and intense loyalties to tribe, clan, and family, to sect and guild; no tradition of local co-operation and initiative could develop, to break the ancient habits of dependence and acquiescence. The liberals tried and failed, and the parliamentary system passed into the hands of those who controlled wealth and could command or buy obedience. They used it chiefly as an instrument to maintain their own power, and to prevent any change or reform which they considered a threat to their interests.

In a long period of tranquillity, the peoples of the Middle East might perhaps have managed to adjust their imported political structures to their own conditions and needs. No such period was allowed to them. Instead, their young and untried democracies were subjected to a series of violent political shocks and stresses, of both internal and external origin, and confronted with the familiar Afro-Asian economic problem of the demographic explosion. In most countries, the parliamentary system collapsed under the strain; all too often, the disappointment and frustration of leaders gave way to a cynicism and opportunism that outraged the moral and religious sense of those whom they professed to lead, and brought the whole institution of liberal democracy into disrepute. For the average Egyptian, representative government means, not Westminster or Washington, but Fārūq and the pashas; who can blame him if he rejects and despises it?

For a while the ideal of democracy was replaced by another – that of republicanism. There was a time when republic and democracy were thought to be two different ways of saying the same thing; modern Greek indeed makes the word *demokratia* do service for both. Today of course we know better; in an age of democratic monarchies and authoritarian republics we are unlikely to confuse the two. Republic and democracy, far from being synonymous, seem barely compatible in many parts of the world.

In the Middle East republicanism has not always been associated with libertarian ideas. The first Muslim republics were established in the Turkic territories of the Russian Empire, where the temporary relaxation of pressure from the centre after the revolution of 1917 allowed an interval of local experimentation. In some areas, notably in Azerbaijan, this took the form of bourgeois nationalist republics, all of which were in due course conquered by the Red Army and incorporated in the USSR. The Kemalist republic in Turkey and the French-style republics in Syria and Lebanon set new patterns, but it was not until after the second World War that a new wave of republicanism was launched with the proclamation of the Egyptian Republic, by the military régime, in June 1953. This was followed by a number of others, not all of the same kind: Pakistan in November 1953 – an Islamic Republic; the Sudan in January 1956; Iraq, by revolution, in July 1958; Tunisia in May 1959; the Yemen in September 1962. Today all but a handful of the states of the Middle East are called republics, though the common designation covers a wide variety of political realities. A republic, in Middle Eastern usage, is a state with a non-dynastic head. The term has no reference to the processes by which the head attains his office, nor to the manner in which he discharges it. Republicanism meant the end of monarchy, and of much – thought not all – that was connected with it. It had nothing to do with representative government or liberal democracy.

While democracy faltered and died in the Arab lands, the quest for freedom entered upon new paths. Political freedom was never much of an issue during the period of Anglo-French domination; though limited in various ways, it was more extensive and better protected than at any time before or since. What was far more important was the demand for corporate or collective freedom, more technically known as independence.

The Anglo-French régimes, by the logic of their own systems rather than in response to popular demand, conceded a large measure of freedom, but withheld independence. It was natural therefore that the national political struggle should have concentrated on the latter and rather neglected the former. The ending of imperial rule was the focus and purpose of all political effort – never more so than in the period just after it was ended. With the coming of independence it was found that freedom – in the old, classical liberal sense – had been lost. There were few to resist or lament its passing.

The ending of foreign rule, when it came, did not solve but merely revealed the fundamental economic, social, and political problems of the Arab lands. Imperialism, though repeatedly vanquished, remained the chief enemy, but with it another was associated – feudalism, sometimes also called capitalism. Both terms designate the existing economic order. A period of experiment and upheaval followed, of policies described by their friends as pragmatic, by their enemies as opportunist. And then, in the summer of 1961, the government of the United Arab Republic revealed the name of the new ideology that was to be their guiding light. It was called Arab socialism, and its purpose was to secure economic liberty, the only kind that mattered. 'Today', said President Nāṣir, announcing a series of nationalizations, 'we are experiencing real economic liberty. No one exercises arbitrary power over the economy of the country or over its inhabitants. Every citizen feels that he is free in his country on the economic level and that he is not subjected to the dictatorship of capital ... True liberty is true democracy. It is economic liberty and social equality.' A few days earlier the president had given his definition of democracy: 'Fundamentally, democracy means the establishment of social justice and equity for the oppressed class as against the oppressive class. Fundamentally, democracy means that government should not be the monopoly of feudalism and exploiting capital, but should be for the welfare of the whole nation ... Democracy is not created simply by issuing a constitution or setting up a parliament. Democracy is not defined by the constitution or the parliament, but is created by eliminating feudalism and monopoly and the domination of capital. There is no freedom and no democracy without equality, and no equality with

feudalism and exploitation and domination by capital'.[13]
Like freedom, like democracy, socialism is a word of many
meanings. The Soviet Union, we are told, is dedicated to the
building of socialism; so too are the British and Scandinavian
Labour Parties. One of the most famous of parties bearing the
name socialist was the National Socialist German Workers'
Party, usually known by its German abbreviated name as the
Nazis. In the demonology of the American right – so we have
been told – socialism means anything to the left of Louis XIV.
According to the rector of Al-Azhar, in a statement published
on December 22, 1961, the most perfect, complete, useful and
profound socialism is that prescribed by Islam, and resting on
the foundations of the faith. To which of these, if any, is Arab
socialism related?

Socialism began in the Middle East with small coteries, as a
rather more recondite version of the prevailing fashion of
copying Europe. A few serious writers gave it their support,
such as the Syrian Christian Shiblī Shumayyil (1860-1917)
and the Egyptian Christian Salāma Mūsā (ca. 1887-1959).
Both followed Western models of socialism, Shumayyil the
French school of Jaurès, Mūsā the English Fabians. Also
French in inspiration was the short-lived and ineffectual Ottoman Socialist Party, founded in 1910, with a branch in Paris
and a newspaper called *Besheriyet* – humanity. The Russian
Revolution brought a brief spurt of left-wing socialist activities
in several countries, but this too petered out in sectarian
squabbling, leaving only a very small, very hard core of professional revolutionaries. In Mandatory Palestine, a strong
social-democratic labour movement, of European type, developed among the Jewish population; elsewhere in the Middle
East, in the twenties and thirties, socialism had virtually no
following – nothing, for example, that could be compared with
the social and political radicalism of the nationalist movements
in India and south-east Asia.

A new phase began with the electoral victory of the British
Labour Party in 1945. Britain, so it seemed at the time, was on
top of the world, and socialism was on top in Britain. Socialism
might therefore be a good thing. In addition, it seemed to provide an answer for the mounting economic problems of the
area. A series of socialist parties appeared in various countries,

the most important of which was Akram Ḥaurānī's Arab Socialist Party, founded in Syria in 1950. In 1953 it was amalgamated with Michel 'Aflaq's Arab Renaissance Party, to form the Arab Socialist Renaissance Party, usually known as the *Ba'th*. This party, with a programme combining economic socialism and a kind of mystical nationalism, soon won a considerable following in the Arab East. Apart from the Communists, it was the only party with a systematic ideology, with an extensive network of branches, and with a following among both the intellectuals and the working classes. In 1956 the *Ba'th* leaders joined the government in Syria, and played a decisive role in taking that country into the United Arab Republic. For a while the *Ba'th* played a predominant role in Syria after the Union, and claimed even to be providing ideological leadership for the UAR itself. By the end of 1959, however, they were losing ground. In Iraq, Jordan and Lebanon they were opposed and, on occasion, suppressed; even in the UAR their leaders were dismissed from the high federal offices which they had held, and the party itself was suppressed twenty-two months after the Union. The *Ba'th* did not return to prominence until the spring of 1963, when the revolutions in Iraq and Syria brought it to power in both countries, and inaugurated a new sequence of collaboration and of conflict with President Nāṣir. In the meantime the only place where Socialist ideology could be seriously discussed was liberal, capitalist Beirut.

Socialism was in the air in the nineteen fifties, as liberalism had been a century earlier. Like its predecessor, socialism won a certain following among intellectuals, but it was not they who brought it to power. The socialist revolution, like the liberal constitutions, was imposed from above – not in response to a popular demand, not by the victory of a socialist or working-class movement, but by the decision of a military régime that had already been in power for nine years. Some practical steps, of a non-doctrinal nature, had been taken earlier. British, French and some Jewish enterprises had been nationalized following the Sinai and Suez expeditions; Belgian assets were added during the Congo crisis. The resulting flight of foreign and minority capital narrowed the field of candidates for what one might call conservative nationalizations; the government, apparently despairing of private enterprise, decided to adopt a more active role in economic life. Statements of the time refer to social justice rather than to socialism, and appear to envisage a kind of limited state capitalism, with a welfare programme. By 1960 socialism was becoming more explicit in both word and deed, particularly with the nationalization of the great Miṣr group of enterprises. The nationalization of the newspaper press in the same year was not a purely, or even primarily economic measure.

The next stage came with the series of decrees of July 1961, establishing state ownership or control over almost all large-scale economic enterprises, taking over, with compensation, all land-holdings above 100 feddans (about 100 acres), imposing drastic income-tax in the higher brackets, and forbidding any individual to own more than £E10,000's worth of shares in a list of named companies. At the same time a series of speeches and articles explained the nature and purpose of these measures, and of the Arab socialism which they exemplified. The need of the country, said Muḥammad Ḥasanayn Haykal, in an authoritative ideological article, was for a comprehensive plan, harnessing the entire energy of the nation, which would ensure the necessary increase in production, while at the same time providing for the immediate consumer needs of the long-deprived masses. In this way, economic growth and social welfare would both be achieved without either the domestic and colonial exploitation of Western capitalism, or the ruthless sacrifice of the present to future generations, as practised by Stalin and Mao Tse-tung.[14] A French politician once said that war is too serious a matter to be left to the generals. The Egyptian officers had already decided that politics were too important to be left to politicians; they now also reached the conclusion that business was too important a matter to be left to businessmen.

'Archaeology,' said Mr Bernard Berenson, 'like all studies pursued with a scientific method, is based on comparison. It is constantly comparing unknown with known, uncertain with certain, unclassified with classified.'[15] It is no doubt in pursuit of the archaeological method, which has served so well in the study of earlier periods of Middle Eastern history, that many attempts have been made to explain and to classify recent

Middle Eastern developments by comparing them with earlier, already classified events, which took place at other times or in other places.

Nasirism in its successive phases, the latest of which is Arab socialism, has been subjected to several such explanations by comparison. Some have sought precedents in the Egyptian past – for there is also an indigenous tradition of state economic action, exemplified in the commercial monopolies of the Mamluk sultans in the fifteenth century, and the land nationalization of Muḥammad ʿAlī Pasha at the beginning of the nineteenth. Others have looked for Western parallels, and, pronouncing a kind of guilt by association, have at different times described the military régime as Nazi and as Communist. To call a movement Nazi, in both the West and the Soviet Union, in most of Asia and Africa, is usually considered an insult. It is not so in the eastern Arab lands, where many leaders make no secret of their war-time sympathy and even association with the Axis. When Qāsim called Nāṣir a Hitlerite, the name was a danger-sign of Communist penetration in Baghdad; this was not part of the Arab vocabulary of abuse, and its appearance as such was evidence of alien influence. In Egypt there were many reports, a few years ago, of the employment of Nazi German experts, particularly in police and propaganda work. The pervasive efficiency of the one, and the strident mendacity of the other, may well have owed something to the example or instruction of Nazi specialists. President Nāṣir himself on one occasion cited and recommended the so-called 'Protocols of the Elders of Zion'.[16]

Nevertheless, one should not attach too much importance to this. Others, on both sides of the iron curtain, have not scrupled to make use of Nazi experts, in different fields, when it suited them to do so. Evil communications corrupt good manners. These Nazi associations would seem to indicate a degree of moral obtuseness in the Egyptian régime of a kind that is fairly widespread in the modern world, but not necessarily any greater resemblance to the Nazi dictatorship than is implied in that.

Charges of communism also rest on rather slender foundations. The Communists, like the Nazis, could count on a sympathetic welcome, for they appeared in the same guise – as enemies of the West. But communism, unlike Nazism, is a fact, not a memory – and this meant both opportunity and danger. At one time Communist influence in the Arab world seemed very great; of late it has diminished, as the attractions of communism are offset by the activities of the Soviet government. In any case, the dangers of either ideology have been greatly exaggerated. No doubt, there are some who would like to follow Hitler's path of military aggrandizement, others who would like to take Stalin's road of ruthless industrialization. But in a region which has neither the military potential of Hitler's Germany nor the human and natural resources of Stalin's Russia, neither is possible.

More recently, comparisons have been made between Arab socialism and that of the Labour and Social-democratic parties of western Europe. Though there is little enough resemblance to the parliamentary socialist parties of affluent Europe at the present day, some affinity may perhaps be traced with the non-communist left-wing socialism of the hungry thirties, of the kind which flourished at the left extremity of the British Labour Party and which, by-passing the fascist-influenced Middle East of that time, exercised so powerful an attraction on the nationalist movements of south and south-east Asia. In this sense, Arab socialist ideologies probably owe more to Harold Laski and the early Nehru than to Stalin or Hitler. But much has changed in the transition to the nineteen sixties – and to the Middle East. The movement has lost its ethical urge and liberal humanism, but retained its angry impatience with parliamentary delays; it has lost its optimistic internationalism, and acquired a new content, deriving from sources and impulses profoundly alien to both the liberal and socialist political traditions of the West.

It is no doubt tempting to try and explain Middle Eastern phenomena in terms of European, or North or South American experience; it may also, within limits, be very useful. But on the whole such comparisons – perhaps analogies would be a better word – obscure more than they explain. No doubt, Middle Eastern societies and politics are subject to the same human vicissitudes and therefore to the same rules of interpretation as those of the West. But since the Middle East has for some time now been under the influence of the West, and has adopted Western outward forms in the organization and expression of its political and social life, it is fatally easy for the Western observer to take these alien outward forms as the element of comparison, and to disregard or misrepresent the deeper realities which they so imperfectly express. The Islamic society of the Middle East, with its own complex web of experience and tradition, cannot adequately be labelled and classified with a few names and terms borrowed from the Western past.

The fight for political freedom has been fought and lost – though as an old-fashioned liberal I find it hard to believe that such a defeat can ever be final. The fight for national freedom has been fought and won – though the triumph of nationalism over imperialism has become a new kind of Middle Eastern myth, in need of seasonal and ritual re-enactment. The fight for economic freedom – meaning freedom from want – is engaged. What the result will be, no one can yet say. It may be that the Middle Eastern socialists, like the Middle Eastern democrats before them, will find their new machine falling to pieces in their hands, and cast it aside in frustration and disappointment; it may be that, learning from the errors of their predecessors, they will adapt it, master it, and make it work. This much is already clear – that whatever its nature and outcome may finally prove to be, economic and political radicalism is a powerful force in Arab affairs, and has given a new drive and direction to Arab nationalism.

CHAPTER IV

Patriotism and Nationalism

EVERY student of Islamic history knows the stirring story of how Islam fought against idolatry, in the days of the Prophet and his Companions, and triumphed, so that the worship of the one God replaced the many cults of pagan Arabia. Another such struggle is being fought in our own time – not against Al-Lāt and al-'Uzzā, and the rest of the old heathen pantheon, but against a new set of idols called states, races and nations; this time it is the idols that seem to be victorious. The introduction of the secular heresy of nationalism, of collective self-worship, is the best founded and least mentioned of the many grievances of the Middle East against the West. It is a melancholy task to chronicle the successive phases of contact, infection, inflammation, and crisis.

It is a universal habit of human societies to divide people into insiders and outsiders, and to find opprobrious names for the latter. The two most self-conscious peoples of antiquity called the rest gentiles and barbarians; medieval Islam and Christendom called each other infidels; to most modern societies the term 'foreigner' combines the worst features of both barbarity and unbelief. An amended Latin tag – 'I regard no alien as a human being' – might serve as the motto of a good deal of twentieth century statesmanship and administrative practice.

In Europe and in other countries of European civilization it has been our custom for some time past to classify ourselves, for political purposes, by nationality. There has been some variation in the use of this term. In English (both British and American) and in French the word 'nationality' or *nationalité* indicates the country or state of which one is a citizen or subject. In German, *Staatsangehörigkeit* – state-belonging – is used in this sense, while the term *Nationalität*, though etymologically akin to nationality, is semantically different, with an ethnic rather than a legal-political sense. Soviet usage has adopted and formalized this distinction. The Soviet visa form, and other documents, have separate rubrics for *Grazhdanstvo*, citizenship, and for *Natsionalnost*, which corresponds in meaning to German *Nationalität* and not to English or French 'nationality'. Apart from these formal differences of usage, different nations and parties have, from time to time, variously stressed the importance of citizenship, descent, language, religion, and other factors in determining national identity. But allowing for all these variations, it remains broadly true that in Europe and the Americas we define our identity and loyalty in terms of nationality – that is, to varying extents, by the polity of which we are citizens, the country we inhabit, the stock from which we are deemed to descend, and the language we speak.

This has not been so in the Islamic world. Descent, language, and habitation were all of secondary importance, and it is only during the last century that, under European influence, the concept of the political nation has begun to make headway. For Muslims, the basic division – the touchstone by which men are separated from one another, by which one distinguishes between brother and stranger — is that of faith, of membership of a religious community. In our day faith is perhaps the wrong word; we all know — from our daily newspapers if not from our own experience — that dislike of other religions long survives any effective belief in our own. What is meant is rather religion as a social and communal force, a measure of identity and a focus of group loyalty.

Within the universal Muslim community, the Muslim accepted as brothers, at least theoretically, other Muslims of whatever language, origin, or place of habitation. He rejected as aliens his own compatriots, who might be of the same stock and speak the same language, but professed another religion. He also rejected his own non-Muslim ancestors, with whom he felt little or no sense of identity or continuity. The neglect of antiquity by the peoples of the Islamic Middle East did not occur because they were barbarous or ignorant, incapable of understanding the importance of such things. On the contrary, they were peoples of high culture, with an unusually strong sense of history, and of their place in it. But for them real history began with the rise of Islam. Their spiritual ancestors were the early Muslims in Arabia and the heartlands; the heathen Egyptians, Babylonians and others were remote and alien peoples, with whom, despite the accidental and unimportant links of blood and soil, they had no real connexion. It was only in the nineteenth century, when European archaeology revealed something of the value of this forgotten past, that they began to take an interest in it – an interest that grew and developed as it became associated with the newly imported Western ideas of the fatherland and nation, of the mystical and continuing identity of a people and the country they inhabit.

The Ottoman Empire was the last and the most enduring of the great Islamic universal empires that had ruled over the Middle East since the day when the first of the caliphs succeeded the last of the prophets. Within it, the basic loyalty of Muslims was to Islam, to the Islamic Empire that was its political embodiment, and to the dynasty, legitimized by time and acceptance, that ruled over it. The discontented and the rebellious might seek a change of ministers, of sovereign – even, in a few cases, of dynasty; they never sought to change the basis of statehood or corporate identity.

In this respect the situation in the Middle East until the nineteenth – perhaps even the twentieth – century was not unlike that which existed in medieval Europe. The greatest poet of medieval Christendom, Dante, in his dreams of reviving a universal Christian Roman Empire, was not disturbed by the fact that the Roman emperors of his day happened to be German and not Italian. Italy and the Italians existed and were of profound importance; but their true political expression was as a part of the universal Christian monarchy. The idea of Italy as a political entity, needing to express its territorial and national identity in statehood, lay far in the future. In the same way, until the impact of European political ideas, the Arab subjects of the Ottoman Empire, though well aware of their separate linguistic and cultural identity and of the historic memories attached to them, had no conception of a separate Arab state, and no serious desire to part from the Turks. Certainly, they did not question the fact that the sultans happened to be Turkish. On the contrary, they would have found it odd had they been anything else. So alien was the idea of the territorial nation state that Arabic has no word for Arabia, while Turkish, until modern times, lacked a word for Turkey. The Turks now use a word of European origin; the Arabs make do with an expression meaning the island or peninsula of the Arabs.

The old order continued to function, more or less effectively, until the introduction of new ideas from Europe began to undermine the firm basis of acceptance on which it had rested. The impact of Western action and example was changing the structure of society and the state; the influence of Western thought and practice encouraged the emergence of new political conceptions, affecting both the pattern of authority in the state, and the basis of association of its subjects. During the nineteenth and twentieth centuries, the old Islamic and dynastic loyalties that prevailed among the Turks, Arabs, and Persians were modified, transformed and, at times, replaced by the disruptive European ideas of patriotism and nationalism, with their new, abstract theories of country and nation to obscure the older realities of state and faith.

Today the three major peoples of the Middle East, the Turks, Arabs, and Persians, have become intellectually isolated from one another. Each is absorbed in its own dialogue with the West, and has little knowledge of the other two, or interest in them, beyond the surface movement of political events. Arabic is still taught as a classical and scriptural language in Persian secondary schools – and conveys about as much contact with Arab movements as the vestigial teaching of Greek in English public schools does with modern Greece. Classical Arabic has also recently been reintroduced in Turkish religious seminaries, and, at a rather elementary level, forms a part of religious instruction among Muslims generally. Apart from this, foreign Middle Eastern languages are studied in the Middle East only by small groups of students in specialist and learned institutions. The general, educated public knows nothing of the other two languages, and is almost totally ignorant of the intellectual and cultural movements expressed in them. Cairo, Tehran and Istanbul have become culturally very remote from each other. They may still look outwards for guidance and inspiration; they do not look to one another.

It was not always so. In the nineteenth century Arabic was still read and understood by most educated Muslims; Turkish was still an imperial language, the medium of communication of the last, great independent Muslim Empire, to which Muslims everywhere looked as their guide and as their final hope. Today a knowledge of Turkish is a rarity in the Arab lands. In Ottoman times it was a language of government and education in the cities of Syria and Iraq, and survived even in Egypt, until yesterday, as a language of the court and aristocracy. Persian was the hall-mark of an educated gentleman in the Ottoman lands; Ottoman Turkish was read and understood by important elements among the Turkic-speaking populations in Transcaucasia, Iran, and Central Asia. Apart from ease of communication, the three peoples were still near to one another in spirit and outlook, and had not yet grown apart into a series of separate, insulated nation-states. New ideas and new moods could still be communicated swiftly all over the Middle East, and it is only in the larger framework of the area as a whole that the separate development of the Turks, Arabs, and Persians can be adequately understood.

Turkey was the most advanced and most powerful country in the region; the Turks were the most sophisticated and experienced nation, with the longest and closest acquaintance with Europe. It was natural that the new ideas should first have appeared among them, and have been transmitted by them to their subjects and neighbours.

Patriotism and nationalism are the words that express the normal kind of corporate loyalty and identity in the modern world. Both are words of unstable and therefore explosive content, and need to be handled with care. The two, in English usage, convey very different suggestions and associations. Patriotism, most of us would agree, is right and good – the love and loyalty which all of us owe to our country. Nationalism, on the other hand, is something rather alien, and therefore rather suspect. The expression 'English nationalism', for example, does not come very naturally to the tongue. One thinks of nationalism as being Celtic or continental, African or Oriental, but not English, nor, I suspect, American.[16a]

The first stirrings of the new loyalty in the Middle East took the form of patriotism, not nationalism. They were inspired by the example of Western Europe, particularly of France and England, where nationhood and statehood were identified, and where patriotism was the loyalty which the citizen owed to his country, and normally paid to the government when it fell due. This new conception, which seemed to reinforce and extend the claims of the state to the loyalty of its subjects, at first received some encouragement from Middle Eastern governments; later they found that the transfer of allegiance from a person to an abstraction raised unexpected difficulties.

The term used to convey the idea of country, or more precisely of the French *patrie*, was the Arab word *waṭan*, which has passed, with some changes of pronunciation, into Persian, Turkish, and other Islamic languages. The primary meaning of *waṭan* was a man's place of origin or habitation, usually used of a town, village or at most a province. A famous book of definitions of the fourteenth century distinguishes between the *waṭan* proper, 'a man's birthplace and the place where he lives' and the *waṭan* of sojourn, where a man spends at least fifteen days but does not establish permanent residence. A man's *waṭan* could be the object of sentiment, affection and devotion, as many passages in classical Islamic literature attest. The ninth-century Arabic essayist al-Jāḥiẓ wrote an essay on affection for one's homeland. The thirteenth-century Syrian geographer Ibn Shaddād begins his work on Syria and Mesopotamia with his own native city of Aleppo, and justifies his choice in an eloquent passage, studded with quotations from tradition and poetry, on the merits of loving one's *waṭan*.[17] An oft-cited dictum, attributed to the Prophet, is that 'love of one's *waṭan* is part of the faith' (*Ḥubb al-waṭan min al-īmān*). The fifteenth century Central Asian Turkish poet 'Alī Shīr Navā'ī even speaks of fighting for one's *waṭan* –

> For family and *vatan* as long as he has life
> A man will fight as long as he can?[18]

From this and from many other passages in which *waṭan* is associated with family affection, memories of youth, and yearning in absence, it is clear that the classical word *waṭan* is the equivalent, not of the French *patrie*, but rather of the English word 'home' in its broader sense. Like 'home', it carries a wealth of sentimental associations, notably in the period of the Crusades, when so many homes were lost or threatened; like it again, it has no political content.

The first example known to me of the use of the word *waṭan* in a political sense occurs in a report of Morali Esseyyid Ali Efendi, Ottoman ambassador in Paris under the *Directoire*, where he describes the way in which the French authorities cared for disabled soldiers – men who had suffered 'in the cause of the republic and out of zeal for the *vatan*'.[19] This was a new idea, and it is doubtful whether Ali Efendi, whose reports do not suggest any great keenness of perception, really understood it. More probably, he, or rather his interpreter, was merely translating literally from a French original, without appreciating its real import.

Nevertheless, the new idea spread, and in 1839 the words 'love of country (*vatan*)' even appear in an Ottoman official document – the famous reform edict known as the Rescript of the Rosechamber. In 1840 the Turkish diplomat Mustafa Sami, in his *Essay on Europe*, speaks of 'love of country' as one of the praiseworthy qualities of the people of Paris, and adduces his own love of country as his reason for publishing this booklet. By 1841 the expression *hubb ül-vatan*, love of country, was sufficiently established in its new meaning to appear as the equivalent of patriotism in Handjeri's Turkish-French dictionary, where it is illustrated with a number of phrases expressing patriotic sentiments. In 1851 the Turkish poet and journalist Shinasi, in a letter to his mother, said, 'I want to sacrifice myself for my religion, state, country and nation' (*din ve devlet ve vatan ve millet*). The Crimean War was the occasion for a more militant patriotism, and the appearance of the first patriotic poem. By this time the word *vatan* was in current journalistic usage; in 1866 it even appeared in the name of a new newspaper – the *Ayine-i Vatan* – Mirror of the Fatherland.[20]

The appearance of patriotic ideas in Egypt came a little later than in Turkey, and was to a large extent the work of Shaykh Rifāʿā Rāfiʿ al-Ṭahṭāwī. During his stay in Paris from 1826 to 1831, he must have become aware of the significance of patriotism in French life, though he makes little reference to it in his book on France. His patriotic writings came some years later, and enjoyed official encouragement. In 1855 he published an 'Egyptian patriotic ode' (*qaṣīda waṭaniyya Miṣriyya*) in praise of the new ruler Saʿīd Pasha, and, in the same year, a collection of 'Egyptian patriotic poems' (*manzūmāt waṭaniyya Miṣriyya*), inspired by the exploits of the Egyptian contingent sent to help the Turks in the Crimean War. Another patriotic ode greeted the accession of Ismā'īl eight years later, and further *waṭaniyyāt*, patriotic poems, appeared in 1868, after the return of the Egyptian, actually negro, battalion from Mexico, where they had gone as part of Napoleon III's expeditionary force.

Shaykh Rifā'a's patriotic poems, some of them in simple, martial verse, sing the praises of Egypt, of the Egyptian soldier and army, and of the Khedivial dynasty. In his prose works he develops his patriotic teachings at greater length, citing the tradition that 'love of country is part of the faith' and the dicta assembled by Ibn Shaddād. Patriotism, for Shaykh Rifā'a, is the bond which holds the social order together; to inculcate it in the young is one of the primary purposes of education. His patriotism is clearly and distinctively Egyptian. It is not Arab, since it does not include the other Arabic-speaking countries; nor Muslim since it *does* include the ancient Egyptians of pre-Islamic times, and even the non-Muslim residents of Egypt in his own day. As far back as 1838 Shaykh Rifā'a had produced the first Arabic translation of a European history of Pharaonic Egypt. In 1868 he tried his own hand at a history of Egypt from antiquity up to the Arab conquest. His later works are full of a sentiment of pride in the glories of ancient Egypt, and of a deep love for his country, which he sees as a living, continuing entity from the days of the Pharaohs to his own. This was a new and radical idea in the Muslim world. It was long before its equivalent appeared in any other Muslim country.

Shaykh Rifā'a's brand of patriotism was sponsored and encouraged by the Khedives, who saw, in the emergence of a distinctively Egyptian political personality and loyalty, a support for their own dynastic and separatist ambitions. Members of the khedivial family also helped, for different reasons, in the launching of another brand of patriotism – that of the Turkish group of liberal patriots known as the Young Ottomans.

The eighteen-fifties and sixties brought important developments. The war had aroused a passionate desire for news and interpretation; the telegraph and the press came to supply them. The strains of the Crimean War and the example of Turkey's Western allies stimulated the growth of patriotism, which found expression in the new and widely read newspaper and magazine press. The Young Ottoman group, formed in 1865 to press for a

more liberal political régime in the Empire, based themselves
from the start on a patriotic as well as a liberal programme.

Namik Kemal, the intellectual leader of the group, wrote
eloquently in both prose and verse on patriotism – on the greatness of his country, and the loyalty owed to it by its citizens. The
first leader of the first issue of *Hürriyet* – Freedom – the journal
published by the exiled liberals in London in 1868, is headed
'*Ḥubb al-waṭan min al-īmān*' – love of country is part of the faith
– a tradition now becoming popular among the new patriots.
The same theme is argued and developed in a series of articles,
published both during his stay in Europe and after his return
to Turkey in 1870. He went into exile again in 1873, following
the too enthusiastic reception of his ardently patriotic play
Vatan or Silistre, celebrating an episode in the Crimean War.

The unit of Namik Kemal's patriotism is the Ottoman Empire
– its sovereign, its territory, its peoples. The word Turk appears
rarely in his writings, and then as a synonym of Ottoman Muslim. The word Ottoman frequently means Muslim, but at other
times refers to all the Sultan's subjects irrespective of religion or
race, who are to be united in a single loyalty. Kemal's conceptions of nation and country are confused, often contradictory,
and change during the course of his career. They are overshadowed by his profound and constant loyalty to his religion.
Despite his use of the terms country and patriot, and his appeals
to his non-Muslim fellow-citizens, the entity which he serves is
ultimately Islamic. This can be seen most clearly in his many
historical writings and allusions. He is uninterested in the history
of Turkey before the coming of the Muslim Turks; he is equally
uninterested in the history of the Turks before their conversion
to Islam. Kemal's *Vatan* was ruled by Arab caliphs as well as
Turkish sultans; its sons include Arab and Persian sages as well
as Turkish heroes. There is nothing in Kemal's patriotism to
resemble the clear sense of identity and continuity of Egypt and
the Egyptians expressed in the writings of Shaykh Rifāʿa. Kemal
was a critic and not a spokesman of the régime, a journalist more
than a teacher, but still a member of the ruling group of an
Empire. The inconsistencies of his ideas are perhaps a measure
of their relevance and their reality, in an age of great changes
still imperfectly understood.

In several of his essays Kemal offers his readers reassurance against the dangers of separatism among the many peoples and races of the Empire. It is true, he says, that the population of the Empire is very diverse; the different peoples are, however, so thoroughly mixed that none of them is strong enough in any region to form a viable separate state or to join an existing one. The only exception is the Arab provinces, which are inhabited by a people of many millions, speaking another language and feeling themselves to belong to another race. They were however Muslims, 'bound to us by Islamic brotherhood and allegiance to the Caliphate',[21] and would not therefore break away in the name of Arabism or the like.

Kemal was wrong on both points, though the proof of his errors lay far in the future. For the time being the Arab provinces did indeed remain bound by Islamic brotherhood and dynastic loyalty, which meant far more to them than the new-fangled notion of Ottoman patriotism. An exception was the Christian Arab *élite* of Beirut and the Lebanon, where patriotic ideas evoked a certain response. As Christians, they were more open to European ideas. But unlike the Christians of Anatolia and Rumelia, they shared the language and culture of their Muslim neighbours, and had no memories of separate national identity. On several occasions, most recently in 1860, they had suffered severely from religious persecution. They therefore had every inducement to favour a patriotic instead of a religious basis of allegiance. If language, culture, domicile and citizenship were to be the criteria of identity, then the Christian Arabs might hope that their possession of the first three would entitle them to the fourth, and give them that unrestricted, first-class membership which they lacked in the Islamic Empire. As early as 1860 Buṭrus al-Bustānī founded a school called *al-Madrasa al-waṭaniyya*, and addressed his appeals for solidarity and loyalty to his Muslim and Christian compatriots. In 1870 he used the formula 'love of country is part of the faith' as motto of his fortnightly magazine *Al-Jinān*. Bustānī writes as a loyal Ottoman subject, but the *waṭan* of which he speaks is Syria – a province of the Empire rather than the whole of it. Some Maronite Christians, angered by Muslim persecution and sustained by memories of Lebanese autonomy, even thought of an anti-Ottoman Lebanese patriotism, similar to the movements of the Greeks and Serbs. These were the only stirrings of disloyalty at that time in the Arab provinces, which otherwise remained faithful to the Ottoman Islamic Empire.

Egypt then, was the only country where territorial, non-confessional patriotism made any headway among a Muslim people. There were many advantages; a country strikingly defined by both history and geography; a vigorous reigning dynasty determined to achieve territorial independence; a splendid ancient past – the first to be rediscovered, and in many ways the most magnificent – to sustain patriotic pride. In 1882 a new and powerful stimulus to patriotic feeling was provided – the British occupation. Even before the coming of the British, the growing feeling against foreigners had found expression in the famous slogan 'Egypt for the Egyptians', launched by the Christian journalist Selīm Naqqāsh, popularized by the Jewish pamphleteer Abū Naddāra, and applied by the Muslim soldier 'Urābī Pasha. During the eighteen-seventies several developments in Egypt had led to mounting resentment and to improved ways of expressing it. On the one hand there were a shallow Nile, a weak and spendthrift government, and growing foreign influence; on the other, an expanding newspaper press, improved education, and an influx of writers and intellectuals from the unfree lands of Islamic Asia – notably the pan-Islamic leader Jamāl al-Dīn al-Afghānī, and a number of journalists, mostly Christian, from Ottoman Syria. In 1879 a group of Egyptians formed *al-ḥizb al-waṭanī*, usually translated the National Party, though Patriotic Party would be a more literal rendering. This was followed, after the British occupation, by a series of other societies, associations and parties, expressing, in various degrees and in different ways, opposition to foreign rule. The most important was the National Party led by Muṣṭafā Kāmil, the political and intellectual leader of Egyptian resistance at the end of the nineteenth and the beginning of the twentieth century.

It would be a mistake to regard these as purely patriotic national liberation movements. The element of Muslim identity and loyalty was still very strong; it was nourished by the contemporary current of Islamic modernism and revival, and sometimes found an outlet in expressions of hostility and mistrust towards non-Muslims. The resistance movements were, however, essentially Egyptian, and concerned with the pursuit of

Egyptian objectives. They were not anti-imperialist – merely anti-British, since Britain was the occupying power in Egypt. Muṣṭafā Kāmil's pro-French attitude was in no way affected by French action in North Africa, just as, earlier in the century, Shaykh Rifāʿa had been unconcerned with the French conquest of Algeria, which began while he was still in Paris. They were not Arab nationalists either. For Muṣṭafā Kāmil and his contemporaries, the greatness of the medieval Caliphate was something in which their ancestors participated, and in which they might claim a share of pride. It was, however, a dead, classical past – much less vivid to them than the newly re-discovered glories of pharaonic Egypt. The Arabs of Asia were foreigners – cousins rather than brothers, and Egyptian writers like ʿAbdallah Nadīm and Muṣṭafā Kāmil at times attacked the Syrians settled in Egypt, whom they called *dukhalā'* – intruders. In so far as their cause was part of a larger one, it was still that of Islam. ʿUrābī's movement had been directed not so much against foreigners as against the Turco-Circassian elements that dominated the army, the aristocracy and the court. Under the British occupation, this cleavage seemed less important; Muṣṭafā Kāmil, criticizing the ʿUrābists, accused them of 'ethnic hostility', and argued that the Turks and Circassians, long established in Egypt, must be regarded as Egyptianized and as part of the nation.

Even in Egypt, the West European type of patriotism had only a limited appeal, and was much modified by the impact of older and deeper loyalties. It had still less appeal in Persia and the Ottoman Empire, which were ruled by established dynasties upheld by traditional Islamic loyalty. Persia was a country in-habited by a nation with a long and distinguished history, marked off from their neighbours by their language and their Shiʿite religion – yet despite the beginnings of a patriotic move-ment in literature, and a nascent interest in the glories of ancient Iran, the majority of Persians continued to think of themselves primarily as Muslims, and of their country as the 'lands of Islam'. Amid the mixed population of the Ottoman Empire, patriotism – that is, Ottoman patriotism – had even less chance of success. All over the Middle East, the essential prerequisites of the Western European type of state and loyalty were lacking. There was nothing like the legal and territorial nationality of

Great Britain or Switzerland, with their long traditions of ordered liberty and corporate identity; nothing like the political and centralist patriotism of France, resting on an ancient identity of statehood, country, language, and culture, and infused, from the time of the Revolution, with new and passionate libertarian ideals. Amid the ethnic confusion, political quietism, and religious collectivism of the Middle East, there seemed little prospect of their emerging.

The ever fertile continent of Europe had, however, more than one example to offer to its neophytes and disciples elsewhere. In central and eastern Europe there were no well-defined and old established nation-states like England, France or Spain. Instead there were nations and peoples, lost in polyglot dynastic empires, divided into small principalities, or subject to alien rule. There were Germans, but no Germany; Poles, but no Poland; Italians, but no Italy; Hungarians, but only a shadow of Hungary. To these peoples patriotism, of the Western European type, had small appeal, for it could only bind them to dynastic or foreign masters, and perpetuate divisions that were becoming unacceptable. Their profoundest loyalty was given, not to state or country, but to the nation or people, and expressed, not in patriotism, but in nationalism. The point was made with characteristic vigour and clarity by Namier: 'Here it was not the state that moulded nationality, but a pre-existent nationality which postulated a State. The German concept of nationality is linguistic and "racial", rather than political and territorial ...' 'The highest forms of communal life became the basis of West European nationalisms, the myth of the barbaric horde that of German nationalism'.[22]

'The myth of the barbaric horde' – a vivid phrase, that can be expressed in Arabic in one word, *qawmiyya*.

This kind of nationalism was concerned first with independence, unity and power; only secondarily, if at all, with individual freedom. 'One reason for dissatisfaction', wrote Prince Chlodwig zu Hohenlohe-Schillingsfürst in 1847 '... is the nullity of Germany vis-à-vis of other states ... It is sad and humiliating not to be able to say proudly abroad: "I am a German" ... but to have to say: "I am a Kurhesse, Darmstädter, Bückeburger; my Fatherland was once a great powerful country, but is now split into thirty-eight fragments."' Most supporters of Arab nationalism would recognize and share the feeling that inspires this remark; most of them, alas, would also endorse the saying of the German liberal leader Bassermann in 1849: 'If I knew the unity and future greatness of Germany were to be attained through a temporary renunciation of all the freedoms, I should be the first to submit to such a dictatorship'.[23]

This kind of nationalism – romantic, subjective, often illiberal and chauvinistic, contemptuous of legal loyalties and neglectful of personal freedom – corresponded much more closely with conditions in the collapsing polities of the Middle East, and in time awoke an overwhelming response among its peoples. As in the countries of its origin, it has aroused passionate loyalties and evoked great efforts and achievements; it has also again led to the loss – one might even say to the abandonment and renunciation – of political freedom.

The new ethnic nationalism came from central and eastern Europe, through several channels. The first carriers were probably the Hungarian and Polish refugees who went to Turkey after the unsuccessful revolution of 1848. Several of them stayed permanently, embraced Islam, and held important posts in the Ottoman service. One of them was Count Constantine Borzęcki, later Mustafa Jelâleddin Pasha, who in 1869 published a book in Istanbul, in French, called *Les Turcs anciens et modernes*. The main part of the book consists of a report and recommendations to the Sultan on the current problems of the Empire. There is also an historical section, including a survey, based on European orientalist publications, of the earlier history of the Turkic peoples, in which great stress is laid on their positive and creative role. Borzęcki is at pains to prove that the Turks are a white race, akin to the peoples of Europe, and belonging to what he calls the 'Touro-Aryan' race.

Count Borzęcki's transposition of Polish nationalism into the Turkish mode was supported by themes borrowed from the works of European Turcology. Some knowledge of the findings of this branch of orientalist scholarship was reaching the Turks through various channels, with significant effects on their conception of their corporate identity and place in history. The Turks, even more than the Persians or Arabs, had forgotten their pre-Islamic past, and sunk their identity in Islam. The

Turcologists – accidentally and incidentally, for the most part – helped to restore it to them, and to launch a new movement, which later came to be known as pan-Turkism. Its main strength was at first not among the Turks of Turkey but among the Turkic subject peoples of the Russian Empire loosely, collectively, and inaccurately called Tatars; these, in their attitudes towards Russia, had gone through much the same phases and moods as the Muslims in India and Egypt towards Britain – of sullen withdrawal, of response and reform, of reaction and rejection. In the schools and universities of Russia, Tatar intellectuals had studied the ancient history and literature of their people, and acquired a sense of pride and identity; they had also encountered the mystical pan-Slav nationalism of their masters, and reacted against it with a pan-Turkism of their own.

Tatar exiles and émigrés from the Russian Empire brought these ideas to Turkey. At first they encountered a cool reception among the Ottoman Turks, who saw no reason to adopt a doctrine which would disrupt the multi-national Empire over which they ruled. The great Turkish poet Mehmet Akif was especially vehement against ethnic nationalism, which he saw as fundamentally unpatriotic and irreligious. But times were changing. The loss of province after province in Ottoman Europe to independent national states reduced the scope and indeed the purpose of Ottomanism; the departure of the non-Turkish peoples increased the relative and absolute importance of the Anatolian Turkish core of the Empire that remained. The idea began to gain favour of seeking a new base of identity – not the crumbling, polyglot empire of the Ottomans, but a new unity based on the mighty and multitudinous Turkish race, stretching from the Aegean across Asia to the China Sea.

These ideas were suppressed under Abdülhamid. They burst into the open after the revolution of 1908, and began to acquire considerable support among the Young Turks. Like the Egyptians, the Turks began to seek sustenance in their past – but it was the past of the Turks, not of Turkey, that interested them. The bounds of historical enquiry were pushed back beyond the Islamization of the Turks, to the ancient history of the Turkic peoples in their central and east Asian homelands. There was still no interest in the pre-Turkish history of Turkey

– in Byzantium, or Troy, or the ancient states of Asia Minor. This did not come until a generation later.

Turkism is thus a form of nationalism, not of patriotism. The focus of loyalty was not the amorphous Ottoman Empire or the effete Ottoman state, but the mighty Turkish family of nations, most of whom lived beyond the frontiers of Turkey, 'the last independent fragment of the Turkish world' as a pan-Turkist once called her. In 1914 Turkey found herself at war, with two great allies, against Russia, the imperial power that ruled over most of the Turkic lands and peoples. For the first time there seemed a serious possibility of achieving the pan-Turkish dream. In the words of the poet-sociologist Ziya Gökalp

> The land of the enemy shall be devastated
> Turkey shall be enlarged and become Turan.[24]

After a period of discouragement caused by the defeats of the Ottoman armies in the field, hope flared again after 1917, when the outbreak of revolution and civil war in Russia, and the collapse of Russian authority in Central Asia and Transcaucasia, seemed to bring the moment of Turkic liberation and unity very near.

In Egypt, patriotic leaders showed an increasing interest in notions of representative and constitutional government, which was still further stimulated by the Persian and Turkish constitutional revolutions. The Organic and Electoral Laws of 1913, and the constitution of 1923, were stages in the development of a liberal programme. Their national loyalty was to Egypt – patriotic rather than nationalist. They took pride in their Arabic language and culture and in their Islamic religion, but rejected both Arabism and Islamism as the focus of identity and loyalty. For the Arabs of Asia – those of them who had not settled in Egypt – they felt a sympathetic interest, based on historical and cultural links, but no common political bond. Their attitude might be described as corresponding roughly to that of an American towards England or, better still, of a Mexican, proud and conscious of his Aztec past, towards Spain. Muṣṭafā Kāmil even condemned the first stirrings of pan-Arabism as a British plot, aimed against the Ottoman Empire and Caliphate.

This kind of secular, liberal patriotism drew its leaders and spokesmen chiefly from the new professional and semi-professional class of lawyers, officials, teachers, and journalists. These, by both their education and their function, were the least traditional and most westernized of all elements in Egyptian society. For this very reason they remained isolated from the vast majority of the Egyptian people, for whose resentments they provided, for a while, an outlet and an instrument, but for whom their aspirations and their ideologies were alien and meaningless. Their failure, disastrous and final, came when their programme of national sovereignty and constitutional government was fulfilled, thus revealing the irrelevance of that programme to Egyptian facts, and its insufficiency for Egyptian needs. Liberal, secular patriotism languished and died during the bitter struggles of the nineteen-forties; its corpse was incinerated on January 26, 1952 – Black Saturday, when the mob burned the centre of Cairo, and destroyed some buildings, a society, and a régime. Among the claimants to the inheritance two predominated – the new pan-Islamism of the Muslim Brotherhood, and the ethnic and communal nationalism of the pan-Arabs, which was spreading from Asia.

Some of the more exuberant exponents of modern Arab nationalism have, at various times, traced its origins back to Muḥammad ʿAlī, to Saladin, to the Caliph ʿUmar, and to Hammurabi king of Akkad. Without attaching too much importance to such flights of fancy, it must be said that the Arab sense of separate identity is very old and deep-rooted. In pre-Islamic and early Islamic times, the Arabs had a strong ethnic and aristocratic feeling, which, in the cosmopolitan Islamic Empire, gave way to a kind of cultural self-awareness based on the common possession of the sacred and scriptural Arabic language. As the philologist al-Thaʿālibī (*d.* 1038) puts it: ʿWhoever loves the Prophet loves the Arabs, and whoever loves the Arabs loves the Arabic language in which the best of books was revealed ... whomsoever God has guided to Islam ... believes that Muḥammad is the best of Prophets ... that the Arabs are the best of peoples ... and that Arabic is the best of languages.ʾ[25] The justified pride of the Arabs in their magnificent language, and in the rich and splendid literature it enshrines, found frequent expression in the course of the centuries. Arabism as a *political* movement, however – as a belief that the speakers of Arabic form a nation with national rights and aspirations – dates only from the late nineteenth century, and it was for long confined to small and unrepresentative groups, most of them Christian. The overwhelming majority of Arabs remained faithful to the Ottoman Empire until it was destroyed. The Arabs were Muslim subjects of a Muslim empire; a popular, national movement such as those that impelled the Christian Serbs and Greeks to revolution and liberty did not and could not arise among them. The small groups of intellectuals who preached an Arab renascence found little response; even the British-sponsored revolt in Arabia was neither as successful in its appeal nor as whole-hearted in its purposes as the official legend suggests.

There were some, however, more significant for the future than for their own contemporaries, who had begun to think in terms of an Arab national revival. As pan-Slavism in the Russian Empire had evoked a pan-Turkish response among the Turkic subject peoples, so pan-Turkism, transplanted from the Russian to the Ottoman Empire, helped to arouse an Arab national feeling among those Ottomans who were Muslim but not Turkish. Political Arabism was born about the turn of the century, and was fostered chiefly by Syrians, especially by Syrian emigrants to Khedivial Egypt such as 'Abd al-Raḥmān al-Kawākibī (1849-1902) and Muḥammad Rashīd Riḍā (1865-1935). The former appears to have been first to come out openly against the Turks and the Ottoman sultan, and to demand an Arab state with an Arab caliph.

After 1918 Arab resentment was directed against less ambiguous and more rewarding enemies – not the Turks and their caliph, but imperialism and Zionism, long familiar under their older names as the Christians and the Jews. Deprived of their old religious and dynastic loyalties, living in artificial political units created by the conquerors, subject to the rule of alien and infidel masters, the Arabs could find little satisfaction in patriotism, and showed little interest in liberalism or socialism, of the kind that flourished in India and south-east Asia. Instead they turned to an ethnic nationalism of central European type, which in the nineteen-thirties drew new inspiration from the central European fountain-head. At first the Egyptians stood aloof from this movement, and were taunted with their 'pharaonism'. Under the military régime the Egyptians, too, have thrown in their lot with Arabism, so thoroughly that the very name of Egypt has been wiped off the map – a result which none of the many foreign invaders and oppressors of Egypt had ever managed to accomplish.[26]

The word which is used to express the notion of ethnic nationalism is *qawmiyya*, an abstract noun formed from *qawm*, meaning, in classical Arabic, people, followers, group or tribe, more expecially the group of kinsfolk mobilized for mutual support. It is in this last sense that the word is used of the North African tribal levies called *goum* – a dialectal pronunciation of the same word. Like *waṭan*, *qawmiyya* is of Arabic etymology, but was first used in its modern political sense in Turkish – the first Muslim language to require and to coin new words for new ideas. In its Turkish form, *kavmiyet*, the word occurs in the writings of the Young Ottomans, as a term for ethnic and local – in other words tribal – nationalities or nationalisms, which conflict with the larger loyalties of the Ottoman sultanate and Islam. Thus in 1870 Ali Suavi criticizes a muddle-headed semi-official Ottoman proposal that the Sublime Porte should, like Italy and Prussia, take up the cause of nationality (*kavmiyet*) and unite all the Muslims. Suavi rightly points out that nationality in Europe means something entirely different. 'Among us there is no problem of nationality. Problems of nationality would cause our ruin. The unification of the Muslims could at most be a question of religion, not a question of nationality?[27] Two years later Namik Kemal wrote an eloquent plea for harmony and unity between the different peoples (*kavîm*) making up the Ottoman Empire, in a common patriotism to their Ottoman *vatan*. He insists that race and religion are secondary to the major facts of country and citizenship, and can best be safeguarded by loyalty to the liberal and tolerant Ottoman state, rather than by breaking it into squabbling and non-viable ethnic fragments.[27a]

Namik Kemal was of course concerned chiefly with the Christian Balkan peoples, and not with the Turks themselves, who were still far from thinking in ethnic or national terms. His appeal was in vain. Nationalism spread rapidly among the Ottoman Christians, and was communicated by them to the Muslims – Albanians, Arabs, and even the Turks themselves. The Albanian national rising in 1912 provoked a passionate rejection from the Muslim patriot, anti-nationalist poet Mehmet Akif, himself of Albanian extraction:

> Your nationality (*milliyet*) was Islam ... what is this
>   tribalism (*kavmiyet*)?
> Is the Arab any better than the Turk, the Laz than the
>   Cherkes or the Kurd,
> The Persian than the Chinese? In what?
> Could Islam be broken up into component parts? What
>   is happening?
> The Prophet himself cursed the idea of tribalism!
>
> The Turk cannot live without the Arab. Who says he can,
>   is mad.
> For the Arab, the Turk is his right eye and his right hand.
>
> Let the Albanians be a warning to you
> What confused policy is this, what evil cause?
>
> Hear this from me, who am myself an Albanian. . . .
> I say no more – alas my afflicted country . . .[28]

Mehmet Akif was fighting a lost cause. He realized this himself when, after a brief association with the Kemalists in Anatolia, during which he wrote the poem that became the national anthem of the Turkish republic, he withdrew to voluntary exile in Cairo. The cause of nationalism spread, ultimately involving all the peoples of the Middle East.

In Persia, a country defined by language, territory and statehood, the identification of nationalism with a kind of Muslim patriotism was fairly easy. A brief interval of racism, due to Nazi influence and to the flattering association of Iran with the privileged and superior Aryans, seems to have had no lasting effects.

In the Soviet Middle East, nationalism has had a more chequered career. After the Russian Revolution, national régimes of various political complexions appeared in Central Asia and Transcaucasia. These were all overcome by the Red Army, and the authority of Moscow restored. Since then nationalism of all forms has been an offence. From time to time reports appear that offenders have been detected and translated, according to the severity of their offences, to other functions, regions, or worlds. The most striking case occurred in 1938, when Feyzullah Khojayev, first minister of the Uzbeg Republic, and Akmal Ikramov, secretary-general of the Uzbeg Communist Party, were charged as nationalists and British spies, and shot. This association of offences, which may seem strange further south, was for long commonplace in the Soviet Middle East. The present strength and direction of nationalism in these lands, like the strength of republicanism in Saudi Arabia, is difficult to assess.

Another brand of nationalism, strikingly different from the Muslim nationalisms in some respects, surprisingly similar in others, is Jewish nationalism, one of the elements contributing to the growth of political Zionism. The corporate self-awareness of the Jews, like that of the Arabs, is as old as their corporate existence; like that of the Arabs, it passed through tribal, ethnic, and cultural phases, to achieve its most characteristic and most enduring form in religion.

Jewish nationalism began in central and eastern Europe, where the unemancipated, unassimilated Jewish communities formed an entity with all the current criteria of nationhood but two – the possession of a national language, and the occupation of a national territory. The Hebrew renascence and the Zionist movement aimed at supplying these two deficiencies. Some substitutes were suggested; the east European Jews did in fact have a language of their own – an archaic Franconian dialect, now known as Yiddish, which they had retained after their medieval migration from the Germanic to the Slavonic lands, and which had developed into a rich and flexible language with a remarkable literature. For a while a kind of Yiddish cultural nationalism found some support, particularly on the left, for the idea of a Jewish secular and popular culture based on the language of the masses. This programme, like the so-called Territorialist movement, which accepted the idea of a national home but wanted to have it in some place more convenient and less troublesome than Palestine, failed to win support among the Jewish masses, to whom their ideas seemed pointless and irrelevant. In the early nineteenth century, the nationalist fervour of the Germans, Hungarians and Poles also involved their Jewish minorities, many of whom felt, fought and died as Germans, Hungarians and Poles, for the German, Hungarian or Polish cause. But the ethnic and often chauvinistic nationalism of these peoples made it difficult for them to accept the Jews as part of the nation; and during the late nineteenth century a sharp cleavage appeared among secularized and national-minded Jews in central and eastern Europe, between those who continued the struggle for acceptance in the reluctant nation, and those who turned away to the idea of a separate Jewish nation in its own homeland – the idea, in a word, of Zionism. For traditional religious Jews, nationalism of any kind was an impiety. For the Jews of the democratic West, the question hardly arose, and Zionism was largely a philanthropic matter. In central and eastern Europe, the modernized Jew, faced with an intolerable situation, was offered a choice between two solutions: assimiliation to the nation, as individuals, or assimilation to nationhood, as a community. The rise of militant antisemitism to a large extent removed the element of choice, and vastly increased the range and force of the Zionist appeal.

Jews are an inventive people. They have been credited, by their more ardent admirers and detractors, with inventing both capitalism and communism, both Christianity and Islam; they did not, however, invent political Zionism, which is in part a Jewish response to the impact of central and east European nationalism, in part an attempt to provide an answer to Jewish needs. Inevitably, like the nationalism of the Arabs, it became intermingled with what was deepest and most deeply felt in the minds and hearts of the people – with their religion, their religious culture and identity, their mystical yearning for Zion. Zionist dreams and aims were focused on two things especially, on Hebrew and Palestine; that is, on a language which the Jews did not speak, and a country in which they did not live. But they were the Holy Language and the Holy Land, both made holy by the Bible, the very core of Jewish existence. This was well understood by the Arabs when they called the Jews *ahl al-kitāb* – the people of the book. Even today, in the secular, nationalist state of Israel, the Jew may be an agnostic or even an atheist, and still pass muster; but let him adopt another religion, and he ceases to be a Jew in any sense that is acceptable to the state, the law, and the overwhelming majority of the people. It may be that, given time, Israel will develop into an ordinary secular nation – she has not done so yet. Perhaps the nearest analogy –

though the differences are great and obvious – is Pakistan, where the attempt is also being made, after struggle, upheaval and partition, to form a new, modern nation based on a religious community.

We have traced the rise and fall of liberal patriotism, the rise and spread of ethnic nationalism. It remains to glance briefly at the most recent phase – the return, still tentative and uncertain, to a new patriotism based on new nation-states that are at last beginning to take root in the consciousness and loyalties of their peoples.

The process began and has gone furthest among the Turks. In 1922, in the moment of victory over the Greeks, they still faced great uncertainties. They were – to borrow a phrase – a people who had lost an Empire and not yet found a new role in the world. In the struggle for national liberation many themes occur – Islam and pan-Islam, Turkism and pan-Turkism, and hostility to the imperialist West. The theme of Turkey – of the fatherland of a nation called the Turks – was for long a comparatively minor one. Yet the form of the struggle, which was to eject foreign invaders from the redefined national territory, inevitably gave it the form of a patriotic war, and prepared the way for a new patriotism, based on an entity hitherto unknown to Turks – the state and land of Turkey. Resisting the temptations offered by the upheaval in Russia, Mustafa Kemal renounced all pan-Islamic and pan-Turkish aims and ambitions, and persuaded his people to do the same. Turkish and Muslim brothers in other lands must fight their own battles; the Turks had urgent and difficult tasks to perform in their own country. Alone among the peoples of the Middle East, the Turks could claim no readily identifiable ancestors in the area in antiquity. Kemal gave them the Trojans and the Hittites, and, through the intensive cultivation of history and archaeology, tried to foster the sense of identity of the Turks with the country they inhabited. By our own day Turkey is well on the way to a patriotism of West European type.

In Israel and Iran also the recovery of the ancient past has proceeded rapidly, and contributed significantly to the growth of patriotism, albeit of a somewhat mythopoeic nationalist tinge. In Israel archaeology has become a national passion, expressing the deep-rooted desire to establish continuity with the ancient past, and to forget the long centuries of the Exile. For the Arab lands the cult of antiquity raised special problems. At first, the revival of interest in the Pharaohs in Egypt was paralleled in the Fertile Crescent – the Assyrians and Babylonians in Iraq, the Phoenicians in Lebanon, the Aramaeans in Syria, were all claimed with pride by the present-day inhabitants of these countries. But soon these movements were drowned by the rising tide of Arabism. The Syrian constitution of 1950 proclaims that Syria is 'part of the Arab nation'. The same formula was later adopted in Egypt, Iraq, and Kuwayt. For the pan-Arabists, the pharaonism, as they called it, of the Egyptians, and similar movements in other countries, were parochial, separatist, and harmful to the cause of Arab unity. These movements were contemptuously designated as Shuʿūbiyya – a reconditioned medieval term meaning, roughly, national factionalism. Sometimes they were actively opposed – as for example in Syria under the UAR, when the Adonis cinema in Damascus was renamed the Balqīs, and any reference to Aramaean civilization was regarded as evidence of support for the dissident, anti-pan-Arab, Syrian Popular Party. At other times they were, so to speak, taken over – as in the attempt to prove that Hammurabi and the rest were Arabs, by the granting of posthumous, honorary Arab nationality to all the ancient Semitic peoples except one. Nationalist historiography is generally worthless to the historian – except the historian of nationalism, for whom it can be very instructive indeed.

At the present time Arabism is the dominant ideology, even in the land of the pharaohs, where the ancient and illustrious name of Egypt itself has been officially abandoned. The reality of Egypt, however, has survived the name, and one of the most fascinating problems confronting the student of Egyptian and United Arab foreign policy is the relative importance of Egyptian and United Arab interests. The same policies can be and have been described as the exploitation of Arabism for Egyptian imperialist purposes, or as the subordination of Egyptian national interests to pan-Arab dreams.

In Iraq, alone among the Eastern Arab states, the position is complicated by the presence of an important non-Arab minority – the Kurds. At one time it seemed that Kurds and Arabs might live together in an Iraqi nation, in the same kind of association as the Celts and Anglo-Saxons in Britain. That hope, and the tolerant atmosphere that bred it, dwindled with the rise of ethnic nationalism, which affected both parties.

The Arab successor states of the Ottoman Empire are now nearly half a century old, and have become familiar and accepted. A complex body of interests has grown up around each of them; all have a strong desire for separate survival. This is especially so where the modern states coincide with ancient distinctions and rivalries, as for example between the valleys of the Nile and of the twin rivers of Mesopotamia. It is noteworthy that, despite the desire for a larger unity, no independent Arab state has disappeared; the first great experiment in unification that was attempted, the United Arab Republic of 1958, ended with the re-emergence of an independent Syria in 1961. The rulers of these countries frequently appear to be guided, in their policies, by the interests of their states and countries rather than those of the pan-Arab cause. But such allegiances and policies, however deeply felt and effectively maintained, are rarely openly avowed. They remain tacit, even surreptitious, while Arab unity remains the sole publicly acceptable objective of statesmen and ideologues alike.

The Arabs are no doubt deeply devoted to the cause of unity, but have not yet decided what they mean by it; whether to follow the path of Germany and Italy to unification – and to follow it where it leads – or the way of the English and Spanish-speaking nations to fraternal association. Meanwhile, though patriotic and nationalistic considerations both influence Arab policies, no one can doubt the immensely stronger appeal of the latter to most Arabs. Patriotism has its claims, but the older rallying cries of faith and kin, now uttered in the new language of Arab nationalism, are infinitely more potent. It is a far cry from the calm loyalty of free men to the country of their birth and the government of their choice.

CHAPTER V

The Revolt of Islam

ON November 2, 1945 political leaders in Egypt called for demonstrations on the anniversary of the Balfour Declaration. These rapidly developed into anti-Jewish riots, in the course of which a Catholic, an Armenian, and a Greek Orthodox church were attacked and damaged. What, it may be asked, had Catholics, Armenians and Greeks to do with the Balfour Declaration?

A few years later, on January 4 and 5, 1952, during the struggle in the Canal Zone in Egypt, anti-British demonstrations were held in Suez. In their course a Coptic church was looted and set on fire, and some Copts killed by demonstrators. The Copts, though Christians, are unquestionably Egyptian – none more than they; and it is certain that no attack on them was intended or desired by the Egyptian nationalist leaders. Yet, in the moment of crisis and passion, the mob in fury felt instinctively that their own Arabic-speaking but Christian compatriots and neighbours were on the other side – and they acted accordingly. For both these incidents there may be explanations deriving from local circumstances. But both undoubtedly reflect an attitude summed up in a tradition ascribed – probably falsely – to the Prophet himself: *al-kufru millatun wāḥida*, unbelief is one nation. Just as Muslims are, in theory, one nation, so too are the unbelievers, and the basic division of the world is into these two groups, the Muslims and the rest. It is in the same spirit that the Algerians found their response to the French slogan of *Algérie française* – not *Algérie arabe*, nor *Algérie algérienne*, but *Algérie musulmane*, Muslim Algeria.

From the beginnings of Western penetration in the world of Islam until our own day, the most characteristic, significant, and original movements of thought have been Islamic. They have been concerned with the problems of the faith and of the community overwhelmed by infidels, rather than of the nation or country overrun by foreigners. The most powerful movements of reaction and revolt, those which have aroused the strongest passions and evoked the widest response, have also been religious or communal in origin and often also in expression. In its long confrontation with the civilization of the West, the Islamic world has gone through successive phases of revival and resistance, response and rejection. Until very recently, it was in religious terms that the problems were formulated, and the different solutions propounded and argued. Even today, it would be very rash to assert that the secularization of Islamic sentiment has passed the point of no return.

An Israeli scholar has defined the difference between the religious and nationalist approaches to events in this way: as believers in a religion 'our forefathers gave praise to God for their successes, and laid the blame for their failures on their sins and shortcomings . . .' As members of a nation, 'we thank ourselves for our successes, and lay the blame for our failures on others'.[29]

The first reactions by Muslim thinkers to the facts of the decline and relative weakness of Islam were, in this sense, religious and not national. In Turkey, a series of memorialists examined the ways in which the state had fallen away from the high standards of the past, and made recommendations on how to return to them. They had little or no effect. The really crucial new developments occurred among the Muslims in India who, during the seventeenth and eighteenth centuries, exercised a little known but very important influence on their co-religionists in the Middle East.

In India, where the Portuguese had arrived at the end of the fifteenth century, followed later by the Dutch, the English, the French, and others, there was an authentic religious revival, which brought new life and vigour to the Islamic faith and community. It was associated with the Naqshbandī order, a Sufi brotherhood of Central Asian origin, which became the vanguard of renascent Islamic orthodoxy. Islam in India was gravely weakened by laxness, heresy and eclecticism; it was threatened both by the insidious return of Hinduism and by the militant Catholicism of the Portuguese. The great religious teacher Shaykh Aḥmad Sirhindī (1564-1624), concerned with the eclecticism of Akbar rather than with any direct infidel threat, tried to show how a measure of mystical faith could be combined with the intellectual discipline of orthodox theology and the social discipline of the holy law. An outstanding figure among his successors was Shāh Walīullāh of Delhi (1703-1765), whose lifetime coincided with the collapse of Muslim power and morale in India, following the break-up of the Mogul Empire, and who, like Sirhindī, tried to bring new unity and vigour to the faith at a time of division and discouragement.

The militant revivalism of the reformed Naqshbandī order spread to the Middle East, to which it was brought from India. As early as 1603-4 the Indian Shaykh Tāj al-Dīn Sambalī, a rival of Sirhindī and a co-disciple of his central Asian teacher, settled in Mecca, where he translated a number of Naqshbandī works from Persian into Arabic. Other disciples and preachers followed. Such, for example, was Murād al-Bukhārī (1640-1720), a native of Central Asia who went to India in his youth and was initiated there into the Naqshbandī order. He later travelled extensively in Turkey and the Arab lands, settling in Damascus in about 1670. He played a role of some importance in introducing and establishing the reformed Naqshbandī order in the Ottoman Empire. His work was continued by his son and descendants. A contemporary of some importance was the mystic theologian, teacher and traveller 'Abd al-Ghanī al-Nābulusī (1641-1731), a native of Nābulus in Palestine, and a recruit to the Naqshbandī order. He had many pupils. Shāh Walīullāh himself had in several works used Arabic instead of the more customary Persian, thus deliberately addressing himself to a larger, Middle Eastern Islamic public. One of his pupils, Shaykh Muḥammad Murtaḍā al-Zabīdī of Bilgram (1732-1791), went to Arabia and then to Egypt, where he made an important contribution to the revival of Arabic learning towards the end of the eighteenth century. Shāh Walīullāh's son Shāh 'Abd al-Azīz continued his work. One of his pupils was the Kurdish Shaykh Khālid Ḍiyā al-Dīn al-Baghdādī (1775-1826), who visited India in 1809.

Shāh Walīullāh himself was strongly drawn to Arabia and the Arabs. 'We are strangers in this land (of India)', he wrote in his testament, 'Our fathers and grandfathers came to live here from

97

abroad. For us Arab descent and the Arabic language are causes
of pride, because these two things bring us nearer to the Lord of
the First and the Last, the noblest of Prophets and Apostles ...
We must give thanks to God for this supreme grace by holding
on as much as possible to the customs and traditions of the
ancient Arabs, from whom the Prophet came and to whom he
addressed himself, and by safeguarding ourselves from the penetration of Persian traditions and Indian habits.'³⁰ Arabia, for
him, was the source of the authentic, original Islam, undefiled
by Persian and Indian accretions. In 1730 he went to the Hijaz
where he stayed for a year, studying tradition and Mālikī law
under Arab teachers; in May, 1732, he went on a second
pilgrimage, and returned to Delhi at the end of the year.

Shāh Walīullāh's idealization of the Arabs and their faith,
coming at a time when the empire of their Turkish masters
seemed to be in the last stages of decrepitude, must have evoked
a ready response among his teachers and fellow-students in
Arabia. There is however no direct evidence of influence or
contact between him and his contemporary, Muḥammad ibn
'Abd al-Wahhāb (1703-1787), the founder of the Wahhābī
religious movement. Muḥammad b. 'Abd al-Wahhāb was a
Najdī, who studied in Medina at about the same time as Shāh
Walīullāh, spent some time in Basra, and eventually returned to
Najd. In 1744, with the support of the local amīr of the house of
Su'ūd, he launched a campaign of militant, puritanical revival-
ism. His object was to restore the pure Islam of ancient Arabia,
by removing all subsequent accretions and distortions, notably
the saint-worship and other idolatrous innovations of the Sufis.
The attack was extended to the ordinary Sunni schools, which in
his view were contaminated by heretical practices and ideas. The
Saudi amīrs of Dar'iyya enthusiastically adopted the Wahhābī
cause, and dedicated themselves to promoting it by force of arms.
After conquering much of central and eastern Arabia, they found
themselves, at the end of the eighteenth century, face to face
with the Ottoman Empire. Accepting the challenge, they raided
Iraq, sacked Karbalā, and in 1804-6 captured and purged the
holy cities of Mecca and Medina. The Saudi amīr sent a defiant
letter to the Ottoman sultan, denouncing him as a heretic and
a usurper. The sultan at last took action, and arranged with the
pasha of Egypt to send an expeditionary force to Arabia to

destroy the Wahhābī power. The task was completed in 1818, when the Saudi capital was occupied and the Saudi amīr sent to Istanbul to be beheaded. The Wahhābī Empire was destroyed; the Wahhābī faith however lived on, to enjoy more than one revival, and to exercise a considerable if indirect influence beyond the borders of Arabia.

The Wahhābī movement in the eighteenth century is in many ways significant. At a time when the Ottoman Empire was suffering defeat and humiliation at the hands of Christian enemies, the Wahhābī revolution marks a first withdrawal of consent from Ottoman Turkish supremacy. Though without any conscious or explicit Arabism, it was a movement of Arabs, directed against the predominantly Persian and Turkish ideas and practices that had reshaped Islam since the Middle Ages, and the first considered rejection of the Ottoman Turkish right to govern. The Naqshbandī influence from India had revitalized Arab religion and the Arabic religious sciences; the Wahhābīs, perhaps stimulated by the Indian revival, went a step further and showed the way to an activist, militant attack on the religious and political order which, so they believed, had brought Islam to its present parlous condition. Though the Wahhābī state collapsed, and the full Wahhābī doctrine found few converts in the Middle East, the religious revivalism which it brought influenced Muslims in many lands, and helped to infuse them with a new militancy, in the impending struggle against European invaders.

During the second quarter of the nineteenth century this struggle was engaged in many parts of the Muslim world. Akif Efendi, an Ottoman official, saw the danger clearly. In a memorandum of 1822 he describes the imminent threat to the Ottoman Empire, and urges its people to defend themselves; otherwise they would suffer the fate of the Crimeans and Tatars conquered by Russia, and of the Indians conquered by England, and be reduced to slavery.

The attack, when it came, was not on the central lands in the Middle East, but on certain outlying areas; the resistance was led and inspired, not by sultans or ministers, generals or *ulema*, but by popular religious leaders, who were able to evoke and direct strong passions and great energies.

Three of these leaders in particular are outstanding – the near contemporaries Aḥmad Brelwī of Northern India, Shamil of Daghistan, and 'Abd al-Qādir of Algeria. They have much in common. All three led armed popular resistance to infidel encroachments – Brelwī against the Sikhs and the growing power of the British in India; Shamil against the Russians in Daghistan; 'Abd al-Qādir against the French in North Africa. All three were religious leaders: 'Abd al-Qādir was a chief of the Qādirī order; Shamil of the Naqshbandī order, introduced into Daghistan in the eighteenth century and revived in a militant form only a few years previously; Brelwī was a Naqshbandī initiate and a Wahhābī at the same time. All three won widespread and passionate support and waged a bitter struggle for Islam against the infidel – Brelwī from 1826 to 1831, 'Abd al-Qādir from 1832 to 1847, Shamil from 1830 to 1859. All three were overwhelmed by superior force, and their countries were pacified and incorporated into the conquering empires.

It was in these empires that the next phase in the Islamic response to the West can most clearly be seen – the phase of adaptation and collaboration. In India, where the Muslims were going through another period of defeat and discouragement after the failure of the Mutiny in 1858, a new leader arose in the famous Sir Sayyid Ahmad Khan (1817-1898), the founder of the 'Mohammedan Anglo-Oriental College' at Aligarh, and a pioneer of educational reform and of Islamic modernism. A great admirer of English civilization and a proud and loyal citizen of the British Empire, Sir Sayyid urged his people to learn English and thus open the way to the modern science and knowledge that were necessary for their recovery and progress. True Islam, he claimed, could not be in contradiction with this knowledge and these purposes. Where it seemed so, some reinterpretation of old principles and practices was necessary – much of it of the kind that the late Professor Koebner called 'creative misinterpretation'. It is not surprising that Sir Sayyid found many opponents, especially among the *ulema*, who saw in him a corrupter of Islam and a collaborator with the infidel enemy.

A parallel figure in the Russian Empire was his Tatar contemporary 'Abd al-Qayyūm Nāsirī (1825-1902), who tried to bring to his people the benefits of the Russian language and of European science and culture in their Russian form. A student in a

Madrasa in Kazan, he defied the ban of the *ulema* on learning Russian, and set to work secretly to master the language of the empire of which he was a subject. He taught for several years in Russian schools and colleges, and wrote or translated into Tatar a great number of books on science, geography, and other subjects. He also produced a Russian grammar, reader, and dictionary in Tatar, to help his people learn Russian, the key to modern knowledge. Not surprisingly, he was made much of by Russian orientalists and others, and is still praised by the *Great Soviet Encyclopaedia*, which defends him against the slanderous attacks of bourgeois nationalists. Among his Tatar contemporaries he was known as Uris Qayyūm – Russian Qayyūm.

It was not long before a violent reaction against this form of collaboration with the West began to develop. It was further stimulated by new moves in the expansion and consolidation of Western power. In 1858 the Indian Mutiny was crushed, and the last shreds of the Mogul Empire swept away. In 1868 the Russians occupied Samarkand, and reduced the amīr of Bukhara to the level of a native prince. In 1877 the Turks suffered a humiliating defeat at Russian hands, and in the same year Queen Victoria became Empress of India; in 1881 the French occupied Tunisia; in 1882 the British occupied Egypt; in 1884 the Russians conquered Marv, and appeared on the borders of Afghanistan; in 1885 the Germans established a protectorate in East Africa.

The idea of pan-Islamism – of a common front of the Muslims against the common threat of the Christian empires – seems to have been born among the Young Ottomans, in the eighteen sixties and seventies, and was probably in part inspired by the examples of German and Italian nationalism and unification. Transposed into Islamic terms, this meant the solidarity and unity of all the Muslims – not of the Turks or any other ethnic or linguistic nation, a concept which would have been meaningless to most Muslims at that time. The Young Ottomans speak frequently of the union of Islam (*ittiḥād-i Islām*) as an important common goal of Muslims, and reproach the Ottoman government for its failure to help the Central Asian Khans when they were being overwhelmed by Russia. Bonds with outlying provinces like Egypt and Tunisia must be tightened, and closer relations established with the rest of the

Muslim world, of which the Ottomans are the natural leaders. Namik Kemal's pan-Islamism was more cultural than political, and was linked with the desire for modernization. Since the Ottoman Empire was the seat of the Caliphate, and was the most advanced of the Muslim states and the nearest to Europe, it was the natural centre of the future Islamic union ... 'When that happens, the light of knowledge will radiate from this centre to Asia and Africa ...'[31] Others, like Ali Suavi, preached a more militant brand of pan-Islamism, and in 1876 the first Ottoman constitution formally claims the 'high Islamic Caliphate' as belonging to the Ottoman house.

Under Abdülhamid II a form of controlled and limited pan-Islamism became official Ottoman policy, and a useful weapon in the armoury of the Ottoman state. At home, it helped the sultan in his appeals to Muslim and especially Arab loyalty against liberals, nationalists, reformists, and other dangerous dissidents; abroad, it enabled the sultan's emissaries to mobilize support among Muslims all over the world, and provided a lever for use against the Christian empires if needful.

A more radical and more militant form of pan-Islamism found expression in the stormy career of Jamāl al-Dīn, variously known as Al-Afghānī and al-Asadabādī (1838/9–1897). An Afghan and therefore a Sunnī according to his own statement, in fact a Persian and therefore a Shiʿite, he claims to have spent his childhood and youth in Afghanistan, and received a traditional education in Muslim learning; he then spent a year in India, where he was initiated into more modern studies, and went on the pilgrimage in 1857. Returning to Afghanistan, he spent some years in the service of the amīr, and in 1869 found it expedient to leave for India. This was the beginning of more than thirty years of travels and sojourns – in India and Egypt, in Persia and Turkey; he spent several years each in France and Russia, and he visited London.

The teachings of Jamāl al-Dīn are the expression of a career rather than of an ideology, and do not cohere into any consistent system of ideas. A bitter critic of Sir Sayyid Ahmad Khan and the reformers, he opposed them on emotional and political rather than on intellectual and religious grounds: they would weaken Islamic cohesion and loyalty, and thus serve the infidel imperialist. Jamāl al-Dīn had his own plans for reform and renewal, in some ways strikingly similar to those of Sir Sayyid – but his purpose was to equip Islam for battle, for *Jihād*, and not for equal co-operation. Despite his diatribes against the 'naturist materialism' of Sir Sayyid, his own beliefs were sometimes suspect; some of his writings rather suggest that his insistence on strict orthodoxy was for the masses, and not for the intellectual *élite* to which he belonged. It has often been said that Islam is a civilization as well as a faith. For Jamāl al-Dīn it was a civilization, potentially a world power, and only incidentally a faith; its basic demand was for loyalty rather than piety. The Muslims were to be united as the Germans and Italians were united, and Jamāl al-Dīn passed his life in the search for a Muslim monarch to whom he could be a Bismarck or a Cavour. The enemy from which Islam needed to be saved was Europe, and especially Great Britain, the imperial power in India and Egypt. His references to French and Russian imperialism in Africa and Asia are few and perfunctory. In his search for a political pivot for pan-Islam, he attempted at different times to collaborate with the Khedive, the Shah, and the Sultan, but ran into difficulties with all of them. He was expelled from Persia in 1891, and spent his last years in politely disguised and comfortably-appointed captivity in Turkey.

The work of Sir Sayyid Ahmad Khan and other reformers had important consequences, even among many who rejected both their methods and their objectives; among these consequences were the spread of western knowledge, a growing awareness of the necessity for a reform in Muslim education, and a wider acceptance of the need to reconsider and restate Islamic values in terms of modern concepts and standards. These themes are present in the writings even of the militant pan-Islamist Jamāl al-Dīn, who, despite his bitter attacks on the reformers, shares their desire to modernize Islamic society and the Islamic faith, and thus to make them defensible against the pressure of Western power and the criticism of Western thought.

Far more successful, in the long run, in these tasks than Jamāl al-Dīn was his associate, disciple, and intellectual superior, the Egyptian Muḥammad 'Abduh (1849-1905), for a while Chief Mufti of Egypt, and a leading figure in the intellectual revival of Islam. At first closely associated with Jamāl al-Dīn in his political pan-Islamism, Muḥammad 'Abduh soon began to follow a line of his own. For him, politics, even the central problem of independence from foreign domination, are of secondary importance; patriotism and nationalism are both suspect in his eyes, since they tend to weaken the religious bond of brotherhood which binds all Muslims together, and forms their true identity and solidarity: 'He who professes the Muslim faith, once his belief is firm, ceases to concern himself with his race or nation; he turns away from sectional ties to the general bond, the bond of the believer'.[32]

The first concern of the Muslim, then, is Islam, which educates, civilizes, and identifies him, makes him what he is, and seeks to make him better. But Islam has fallen on bad days; through internal weakness and error, through external pressure and influence, Islamic values have been corrupted and distorted, and must be restored and defended if they are to withstand the attack of Western criticism, and survive the competition of Western ideas. It was to this task, to the construction and elaboration of a system of Islamic principles and values related to the needs and conceptions of his time, that Muḥammad 'Abduh dedicated his life.

A recent book by a professor of Al-Azhar university on the relation of modern Islamic thought to Western imperialism distinguished two main trends, to which the author, drawing on the terminology of our time, gives the names of collaboration and resistance. The collaborationist trend is represented by Sir Sayyid Ahmad Khan and by the Qadiani Ahmadiya sect; the resistance consists of Jamāl al-Dīn and Muḥammad 'Abduh.[33]

Resistance to Christian and post-Christian Western intellectual and spiritual influences was no doubt one of the main purposes of Muḥammad 'Abduh's thought and teaching. His insistence on the need to cast off the accretions of post-classical Islam, and to return to the pure, unadulterated and uncorrupted faith and practice of the early Muslims, is reminiscent of the teaching of the Naqshbandī revivalists and Wahhābī puritans by whom, directly or indirectly, he was certainly influenced. The movement of ideas which he led is indeed known, from this characteristic doctrine, as the Salafiyya, those who follow the *Salaf*, the great ancestors. But Muḥammad 'Abduh was neither a mere fanatic, nor a mere reactionary, and offered his people something more substantial than empty hatred of the infidel, or the mirage of a return to a largely mythical past. While rejecting the excessive subservience to Western civilization of some modernists and reformers, he was perfectly willing to accept modern science and technology, modern methods of education, and even to take account of modern thought as well as knowledge in a reformulation of Islamic doctrine.

Muḥammad ʿAbduh's struggle for Islam was essentially pacific, concerned with religious, ethical and cultural matters, not with politics or war. Armed religious resistance to the domination of the West or of westernized régimes, of a simpler and more militant kind, still flared up, from time to time, in remote or outlying areas. The action of the Sanūsī order in Libya against first the Ottomans and then the Italians; the revolt of the Mahdī in the Sudan against Turco-Egyptian rule and European encroachment; Māʾ al-ʿAynayn in Mauritania and the Mad Mullah of Somaliland are all examples of such movements, reminiscent of Shamil, ʿAbd al-Qādir, and Ahmad Brelwī in the first half of the nineteenth century. It is noteworthy that all of them occurred in Africa, by now the main area of Western colonization.

In the central lands of the Middle East, religious militancy was less in evidence. It played some part, in different forms, in Abdülhamid's officially sponsored version of pan-Islamism, in the Egyptian national movement, and in the Persian constitutional revolution. It was not, however, a major factor in any of them, and in the political programmes of the radical *élites* of the time was overshadowed by liberal and patriotic ideologies. Religious hostility to the West, and still more to westernizing reformers, smouldered on, however, and burst into flames in the counter-revolutionary mutiny which broke out in Istanbul on April 12, 1909. Some days previously, on April 5, a meeting was held in the Santa Sophia mosque, at which a body named 'the Muhammadan Union' was formed. A journal, named *Volkan*, was launched to propagate its ideas; these, described as a 'revolutionary Islamic internationalism', consisted of a combination of extreme Muslim orthodoxy, militant pan-Islamism, and hostility to the Young Turks and all they represented. The leader of the group, and editor of its journal, was a Bektashi dervish from Cyprus, called Vahdeti. The men of the Muhammadan Union did not confine themselves to meetings and journalism, but played some part in the mutiny of the First Army Corps. The programme of the mutineers and their supporters was simple: 'The *Sharīʿa* (Holy Law) is in danger; we want the *Sharīʿa*!' They did not, they said, want college-trained officers (*mektepli zabit*).

The mutiny was suppressed and its leaders put to death. The question of religion, however, remained in the forefront of Turkish concerns, and played an important part both in the intellectual controversies and in the political conflicts of the Young Turk period. The journals and magazines of that time, which combined a large measure of freedom with a high level of scholarship, contain what are probably the best-informed and best-argued discussions that have yet occurred between conservatives and modernists, and between the different groups within each camp. The militant reaction for the most part remained under cover, occasionally breaking out, as in the unsuccessful conspiracy of 1910, led by the gendarmerie officer Ali Kemal, for the overthrow of the godless Young Turks and the restoration of the *Sharīʿa*.

The First World War, with its secondary conflict between the German-made Ottoman *jihād* and the British-made Arab revolt, brought some confusion in the sentiments and loyalties of Muslims, who were in any case overawed by the immense military power of the two groups of European belligerents. A change began to occur towards the end of the war, and it developed rapidly in the immediate post-war period. It was to some extent prepared by the revolutions in Russia, which seemed to portend the collapse of capitalist European civilization. It was much helped by the disillusionment of the leaders of the Arab Revolt, even to the point of secret approaches to their Ottoman masters, now enemies – yet co-religionists. The German general Liman von Sanders mentions in his memoirs that in late August 1918 the Sherif Fayṣal sent a secret message to Jemal Pasha warning him of the impending British offensive and offering to go over to the Turks in return for certain guarantees for the formation of an Arab state.[34] It is ironic that this proposal was rejected in the quite mistaken belief that it was a British-inspired ruse.

In the days of despair and anger that followed the Ottoman surrender, Islamic loyalties were very strong, and it was to these loyalties that the first calls to resistance were addressed. Even the Communists, in their attempt to win support in Muslim lands, found it expedient to appeal to Islamic rather than to class or national solidarity, and co-operated, uneasily and uncertainly, with the exponents of pan-Islam, whom they tried to use for their own purposes. Despite their secularism and nationalism, the Young Turks had not disdained to play the pan-Islamic card when it suited them, and Enver Pasha had in 1918 launched the grandiosely named 'Army of Islam' for the liberation of the Muslims of the Russian Empire. After the defeat, the Young Turk leaders settled in Moscow, now the main centre of opposition to Western Imperialism, and they busied themselves with plans for a Muslim international revolutionary movement. In 1921 a Congress of the Union of Islamic Revolutionary Societies, presided over by Enver Pasha, was held in Berlin and Rome. Its Communist inspiration was clear.

The alliance between Communism and pan-Islamism, always uneasy, was of brief duration. Enver Pasha, sent to Central Asia to further the cause of the Soviets, joined their nationalist opponents, and was killed in 1922 fighting the Red Army. Sultan Galiev, the Tatar schoolmaster who worked with Stalin at the Commissariat of Nationalities in 1918 and conceived the idea of a revolutionary international of colonial peoples independent of the Comintern, was arrested in 1923 for 'nationalist deviations' and disappeared in a later purge.

The most important and only successful movement of resistance to the conquering and victorious West was in Anatolia, where a group of rebels, led by Mustafa Kemal, defied the Allies, the Greeks, and the subservient Ottoman government. The later secularism and nationalism of the Kemalists has obscured the strongly Islamic character of the movement in its earlier stages, when its declared purposes were to free 'Islamic lands' and 'Islamic populations' – to liberate the sultan-caliph and eject the infidel invader. Muslim religious leaders, from both the *ulema* and the dervish brotherhoods, were prominent among the founders and early supporters of the movement.

There were three of them among the nine sponsors of the famous 'Society for the Defence of the Rights of Eastern Anatolia', founded in Erzurum in the summer of 1919; one of them was a shaykh of the Naqshbandī order. When the first

Grand National Assembly met in Ankara in 1920, 73 of its 361 members were professional men of religion, including 14 muftis and 8 leaders of dervish orders. In February 1921, the shaykh of the Sanūsī order in Libya, who had joined the Kemalists three months previously, presided over a pan-Islamic congress in Sivas, at which many Arab delegates were present. In March 1921, the Grand National Assembly adopted as national anthem the first two stanzas of a deeply religious poem by Mehmet Akif, the anti-nationalist 'poet of Islam', who had gone to Anatolia to join the resistance. In April 1921, in occupied Istanbul, a religious service was held in honour of the martyrs that had fallen in the holy war in Anatolia, and a young, westernized Turkish intellectual, under the strain of great emotion, was moved to reflect that the true home of his people was not 'the national club, the cultural lecture, the political meeting', but the mosque and congregation, 'the house, home, and fatherland' of this nation. This is strikingly reminiscent of the remark of the Grand Vizier and Islamic revivalist Mehmed Said Halim Pasha a few years previously, in 1917, that 'the fatherland of a Muslim is the place where the *Shari'a* prevails'.[35]

The mood changed, however. The sultan-caliph in Istanbul refused to be liberated, and he and his *ulema* hurled anathema at the rebels in Anatolia. Islam, for the moment, became identified with social reaction and political acquiescence. The Kemalists turned from religious to nationalist appeals, and went far on the road to secularization. Their secularism was, so to speak, sanctified by success.

Alone among the defeated powers of the First World War, the Turks had succeeded in defying the victors and obtaining a negotiated peace on their own terms. Alone among the crushed people of Asia, the Turks had been able to drive out the invader and restore full national sovereignty. The effect of their successes was comparable with that of the Japanese victory over Russia a generation earlier. The Japanese had taught the lessons of modernism and liberalism; the Kemalist Turks demonstrated the merits of secular nationalism, and a new generation of leaders in the Arab lands and elsewhere was encouraged to defy the West and follow their example. None were able to repeat their success.

During the nineteen-twenties and thirties the prevailing forms of expression of political loyalties, opinions, aspirations and interests were Western – mostly secular political parties which issued programmes and procured votes. The most important religious movement was still the *Salafiyya*, the leadership of which had passed from Muhammad 'Abduh to his disciple Rashid Ridā (1865-1935), a Syrian settled in Egypt. His very considerable theological achievements and intellectual influence were for long without direct political consequences. At the same time, the attempt in 1925 of Shaykh 'Alī 'Abd al-Rāziq, probably under the influence of Turkish secularism, to separate religion from politics failed utterly, against the entrenched opposition of Al-Azhar.

The beginnings of a more active and general concern with religion can already be seen in the thirties, in the wave of popular literary works extolling Muhammad and the early heroes of Islam. Notable among these was the biography of the Prophet by Muhammad Husayn Haykal, which was published in 1935 and at once won immense popularity. The lives of the Prophet and of the caliphs were also celebrated in a widely-read series of romantic works by the famous author and man of letters Tāhā Husayn.

During this period a number of religious leagues, clubs, and organizations were founded, with Islamic programmes ranging from a vague, generalized expression of piety to a more or less direct formulation of *Salafiyya* doctrines. One of these, the Association of Algerian Ulema, formed in Algeria in 1931, acquired considerable influence and importance. In the Middle East their role was, until about 1945, minor and insignificant, being confined to social and cultural activities without political content or direction.

The ending of the war and the resulting relaxation of Western pressures in 1945 were followed by a sudden and tremendous upsurge of religious movements, expressing a messianic radicalism of a kind familiar and recurrent in the Islamic world from the days of the medieval Carmathians and Assassins to those of Shamil of Daghistan and the Mahdī of the Sudan. During the war years great armies had camped and fought in the lands of the Middle East, involving its peoples in the provision of their needs and the pursuit of their struggles, enriching some and disrupting the lives of others. While the great armies were still there, the expression of the resulting strains and stresses was necessarily muted; as the armies began to withdraw, accumulating resentments and hostilities sought and found new outlets.

Within a very short time, the secular, political nationalist and patriotic movements had outdated and discredited themselves by their very successes. In achieving their classical objectives of political sovereignty and constitutional government, they had shown how hollow and inadequate these were; by really winning the support of the nation – and not merely of a dominant but unrepresentative minority – they had revealed the gap between their own Europeanized political style and ideologies, and the deeper feelings and desires of the people they claimed to represent. Before long, in one country after another, they were swept aside by new movements, of a new kind.

In the thirties and early forties Fascism and Nazism had, to many, offered a seductive alternative to Western liberalism – an ideology that combined the merits of being opposed to the Western way of life, to the Western group of powers, and of being supported by an immensely strong anti-Western military bloc. In 1945, however, Fascism was discredited by military defeat; the more or less Fascist groups and associations of the Middle East broke up or changed their tune, and their leaders looked for other ways. Russia, still reeling from her mighty struggle with the *Wehrmacht*, was not yet able to provide them.

For the past hundred and fifty years, Europe had provided both the objects of resentment, and the ideological means of expressing it. Even now, there were some who began to look to the Western doctrine of socialism as the ideological inspiration of the next phase of anti-Western struggle. But far more significant, in the late forties and early fifties, were the religious leagues, whose passionate reassertion of Islamic beliefs, values and standards responded far more closely to the feelings of the suppressed lower classes, in revolt against their own westernized masters and exploiters as much as against the West itself.

The most active and most successful of these leagues was the Muslim Brotherhood – *al-Ikhwān al-Muslimūn* – a widespread, semi-secret association with a cellular organization, paramilitary youth-groups, and an extensive network of educational and even economic activities and enterprises. Founded in the nineteen twenties by an Egyptian secondary school teacher called Shaykh

Ḥasan al-Bannā' (1906-1949), who was known as the Supreme Guide – *al-Murshid al-'Āmm*, the movement grew steadily but quickly during the thirties, and turned to direct political action in the forties.

The Muslim Brotherhood were soon able to play an important and stormy role in Egyptian politics, especially in the crucial period between the end of the war and the consolidation of the military régime. For a while they operated almost as a new political party, enjoying the support of King Fārūq against the Wafd. In 1948 their volunteer groups fought in the Palestine War; on their return to Egypt they are said to have plotted a march on Cairo and a *coup d'état*, in order to overthrow both the government and the monarchy and replace them by a theocratic republic. The Prime Minister, Nuqrāshī Pasha, struck first. In a series of moves beginning on December 8, 1948, he disbanded the Brotherhood, dissolved its branches, impounded its assets, and arrested many of its members. Three weeks later, on December 28, he fell to the bullet of an assassin who was certainly a member of the Brotherhood, though perhaps not acting under orders. On February 12 Shaykh Ḥasan al-Bannā' himself was murdered, in circumstances that have never been fully explained.

A period of intense underground activity followed, during which the new Supreme Guide Ḥasan al-Ḥuḍaybī took office. In 1951 the Brotherhood were allowed to recover some of their possessions and resume overt activities. They played a role of some importance in the struggle against the British in the Canal Zone, and in the cataclysmic events that led to the revolution of 1952. After a period of uneasy collaboration between the Brotherhood and the military régime, relations deteriorated rapidly. An unsuccessful attempt on the life of Colonel Nāṣir on October 26, 1954 was followed by the outlawing of the organization and the trial and conviction of its leaders, seven of whom were sentenced to death. The sentence on the Supreme Guide was commuted on the grounds of age; the other six sentences were promptly carried out. The University of Al-Azhar, in a statement issued on November 17, 1954, accused the Brotherhood of having 'crossed the limits fixed by God in revelation between good and evil'.[36]

The public image of the Brotherhood – partly though not

wholly of their own making – is one of explosive violence and blind, embittered fanaticism. There is also a positive side, deriving its inspiration from the teachings of the *Salafiyya*, which has been described by Professor Cantwell Smith in these terms:

> To regard the Ikhwan as purely reactionary would, in our judgment, be false. For there is at work in it also a praiseworthy constructive endeavour to build a modern society on a basis of justice and humanity, as an extra-polation from the best values that have been enshrined in the tradition of the past. It represents in part a deter-mination to sweep aside the degeneration into which Arab society has fallen, the essentially unprincipled social opportunism interlaced with individual corrup-tion; to get back to a basis for society of accepted moral standards and integrated vision, and to go forward to a programme of active implementation of popular goals by an effectively organized corps of disciplined and devoted idealists. It represents in part a determination to sweep aside the inactive reverence for an irrelevant, static, purely transcendental ideal; and to transform Islam from the sentimental enthusiasm of purely inert admirers or the antiquated preserve of professional traditionalists tied in thought and practice to a bygone age, into an operative force actively at work on modern problems.[37]

Unfortunately, these aspirations, like so many others, have been frustrated by an inability to confront the realities of the modern world, to examine its problems on the level of modern thought, and to devise solutions within the range of possible accomplishment. As all too often, ignorance and anger have found an outlet in pointless and destructive violence – the ex-pression of a state of mind, rather than of a purpose.

The same combination of idealism and violence, of piety and terror, can be seen in the Persian organization known as the *Fidāī'yān-i Islām* – the devotees of Islam, which, significantly, borrows a term used by the medieval emissaries of the Old Man of the Mountain. Though Shi'ites, they hold pan-Islamic opinions rather similar to those of the Egyptian brothers, with whom they have contacts. On March 7, 1951, one of their members shot and killed the Persian Prime Minister General

Razmārā. It was a visit of the Fidā'ī leader, Nawāb Ṣafavī, to Egypt in January, 1954, that touched off the first serious and open clash between the Brotherhood and the military régime. Recently in eclipse, the Fidā'īs have remained an uncertain and disturbing factor in Persian politics.

Even in Turkey – in the westernized, secularized, and sophisticated society of the Kemalist republic – militant religious opposition to the Kemalist revolution has not been lacking. Its leadership has usually come from the dervish brotherhoods rather than from the official *ulema*. During Kemal's lifetime the spearhead of the religious reaction was the Naqshbandī order, members of which led several armed revolts, notably those in the south-eastern provinces in 1925, and in Menemen in 1930. More recently, the Tijani and Nurju movements have preached and campaigned against the Kemalist revolution, though stopping short of armed revolt.

In recent years these militant religious organizations appear to have lost ground, and in many countries they have been outlawed or restricted. There can be little doubt, however, that they continue to work in secret, or that they respond to the mood and desires of a great many people among the submerged classes in Islamic society. Even the governments, however modern and secular, have often found it useful or expedient to take account of Islamic sentiments and loyalties; the pandering to the Turkish reaction by the late Adnan Menderes, and the use of the Islamic Congress by the government of the UAR, are two different examples. The Lebanese troubles of 1961 began to bear a disquieting resemblance to the communal conflicts of other times and places – sufficient to alarm many Christians, and to join Orthodox and Maronite in an uneasy and unaccustomed alliance. Non-Muslims generally have found it wiser to accept a much reduced role in political and economic life; some have expressed alarm – though rarely in public – at the rising note of fanaticism that is now so often heard.

The most militant and successful organ of the radical reaction, the Muslim Brotherhood, has been suppressed in Egypt. It continues to flourish, despite occasional repressions, in several other Arab lands to which it had spread. Even in Egypt it is by no means extinct, and there are some – rather pessimistic – observers who believe that the Brothers and the Communists – the two organized revolutionary oppositions – are for the time being the only serious alternatives to the present form of government. A distinguished Arab historian, Professor Nabīh Amīn Fāris, has gone so far as to say of the Brotherhood that 'its idea and ideals continue to represent the innermost aspirations of Muslims from Morocco to Indonesia'.[38]

This much is obvious. Of all the great movements that have shaken the Middle East during the last century and a half, the Islamic movements alone are authentically Middle Eastern in inspiration. Liberalism and fascism, patriotism and nationalism, communism and socialism, are all European in origin, however much adapted and transformed by Middle Eastern disciples. The religious orders alone spring from the native soil, and express the passions of the submerged masses of the population. Though they have all, so far, been defeated, they have not yet spoken their last word.

CHAPTER VI

The Middle East in International Affairs

FOREIGN policy is a European concept. It arose in a world of multiple sovereign states, separate but interacting, engaged in multi-lateral and continuous diplomacy. Like most of the paraphernalia of modern public and political life, it is alien and new in the world of Islam.

For the Muslims of classical times, Islam was the one true, final, and universal religion. Ultimately all mankind would adopt it; in the meantime they must be made to recognize the supremacy of the Muslims and the sovereignty of the Muslim state. The world was divided into two – the house of Islam (*dār al-Islām*), where the true faith prevailed and the Muslim caliph ruled, and the house of war (*dār al-ḥarb*), where unsubjugated infidels still remained. Between the two there was a perpetual and inevitable state of war, which might be interrupted by a truce, but could never be ended by a peace. It would end only when the whole world was brought into the house of Islam. To achieve this, the waging of holy war (*jihād*) was a collective obligation (*farḍ kifāya*) of the Muslims as a whole, and a prime responsibility of their sovereign. In the Muslim world there was only one state – the Caliphate, and only one sovereign – the caliph, the rightful, lawful chief of the Islamic community and head of the house of Islam.

For nearly a hundred years this world view was sustained by reality. Islam was a single state and empire, ruled by a single head; it was advancing with giant steps, and seemed well on the way to bringing the whole world within its grasp. There was no reason to doubt the rapid completion of the processes of conquest and conversion by which infidels became subjects, and subjects became converts. The change began with the failure of the last great Arab assault on Constantinople, in the grand style, in 718. This, far more than the better known battle of Tours and Poitiers, marked the limit of Arab expansion, and forced the gradual acceptance of the idea that there was such a limit. In time, the Arabs came to realize that they would not conquer and absorb the Byzantine as they had conquered and absorbed the Persian empire. The capture of Constantinople was postponed to an eschatological future. The late Umayyad and Abbasid caliphs became reconciled to living with a more or less stable frontier, and a continuing power on the other side of it. Before long they also had to accept the fact of division *within* the frontier – of the emergence of hereditary, autonomous Muslim states, giving only token recognition to the caliph.

The reality had changed – but the idea remained. Islamic jurists, deeply influenced by the events and ideas of the early formative phase, remained committed to the conception of the unitary and universal sovereignty of the caliph; they were in consequence unable to equal even the tentative gropings of medieval Christendom towards an international law. There was only one caliph; the question of relations between Muslim states could not therefore in principle arise. When it did, it was either ignored by the jurists, or treated casuistically under the heading of dealings between the caliph and a powerful rebel. Relations with the infidel could, in theory, consist only of *jihād*, interrupted by short truces.

Just as the house of Islam was one, so there was a tendency to treat the house of war as one. According to a tradition dubiously attributed to the Prophet, *al-kufru millatun wāḥida* – 'unbelief is one nation'. This proposition, historically speaking, is patently false. Nevertheless it expresses an important psychological truth concerning the Muslims. The really important division was between believers and unbelievers; the lesser sub-divisions among the latter, particularly those of them who lived beyond the Muslim frontiers, were without interest or significance for Muslims. A noteworthy illustration of this attitude may be seen in the Arabic historians of the time of the Crusades, who rarely bother to distinguish between the different crusading states and nations, but lump them all together under the generic name of Franks. The same term was still in use among the Ottomans, and has survived to our own day.

As long as the Ottomans retained overwhelming military power, they did not need to concern themselves with the trivial factions among the enemy, and the question of a foreign policy hardly arose. It was sufficient to meet and defeat them in battle, and dictate terms to them, to last until the next stage in the inevitable and necessarily victorious advance of Islam.

A change began in the sixteenth century. In 1529 the Ottoman armies withdrew after failing to take Vienna, and settled down to the long and bloody stalemate in Hungary. In Istanbul, the diplomatic representatives of the European powers began their long and intricate contest for positions of commercial and political advantage; in 1535 the Sultan signed a treaty of commerce and friendship with the King of France, to whom alone, among the monarchs of Christendom, he conceded the sovereign title of Pādishāh. In 1606, in the treaty of Sitvatorok, he conceded it also to the Habsburg Emperor, hitherto described in Ottoman documents as the 'King of Vienna'. For the first time this was not a truce dictated by the victors in their capital, but a treaty negotiated between equals on the frontier.

The seventeenth century began with a concession of equality; it ended with an admission of defeat. The second failure at Vienna in 1683 was followed by a series of military disasters; in the peace of Carlowitz, of 1699, the Ottoman Empire was compelled, for the first time, to sign a treaty on terms imposed by a victorious enemy. For the first time, too, the Ottomans tried to use the processes of diplomatic negotiation and the good offices of friendly neutrals to secure some alleviation of the penalties of defeat. The foreign policy of the Ottoman Empire was beginning to take shape.

During the sixteenth century a functionary appears in the government in Istanbul called the Chief Secretary, *Reis ül-Kuttâb*, usually known as the Reis Efendi, and concerned with foreign affairs. He was a comparatively minor functionary, and foreign affairs were only one of his concerns. During the seventeenth and eighteenth centuries he gains in rank – and foreign affairs bulk larger among his preoccupations. He was assisted by the Chief Dragoman. In earlier days this was usually a renegade European Christian; from the mid-seventeenth century the office was monopolized by the aristocratic Greek families of the Phanar quarter of Istanbul, who brought it almost to the level of a ministry of foreign affairs.

Yet in spite of these developments, the notions of foreign policy and international relations remained alien to the Ottomans – and perhaps the best proof of this is their willingness to entrust these matters to members of the Christian Greek minority. The number of European resident embassies in Istanbul was increasing – but the Ottomans were content to send an occasional special mission to Europe, and made no attempt to establish resident embassies until 1793, when Yusuf Agah set up house in London.

A few years previously, the Ottomans had made their first essays in the European power game. The Empire was at war with Russia and Austria; it seemed a good idea to conclude treaties with Sweden, which was also at war with Russia, and Prussia, which could bring useful pressure to bear on Austria. Treaties with these two countries were signed in 1789 and 1790 respectively. The idea of a military alliance with Christian powers was new and, to some of the *ulema*, unacceptable. The military judge Shanizade Efendi denounced it as contrary to holy law, citing as authority the Qur'anic verse ' O you who believe! Do not take my enemies and your enemies as friends! (Qur'ān lx.1).' He was overruled by the Chief Mufti, who cited the tradition that 'God will help the cause of Islam with men who are not of it', as well as other legal texts and arguments.[39]

The lesson was quickly learnt. Only a few years later, in 1798, the Empire was invited to join the coalition against the new menace of the French Revolution. The Reis Efendi, Ahmed Atif, in a memorandum presented to the Divan, recommended acceptance, but remarked: 'Every state must have two kinds of policy. One is the permanent policy, which is taken as the foundation of all its actions and activities; the other is a temporary policy, followed for a period, in accordance with the requirements of the time and circumstances. The permanent policy of the Empire is to prevent any increase in the strength of Russia and Austria, which by virtue of their position are its natural enemies, and to be allied with those states which might be able to break their power and are thus the natural friends of the Empire. But in the present time and circumstances, the policy more conducive to the interests of the Empire is first, to exert its strength to extinguish this fire of sedition and evil and then, this purpose having been accomplished, to act once more as required by its permanent policy'.[40]

In the course of the nineteenth century the main lines of the 'permanent policy' of Turkey were confirmed by practice and experience. Russia, advancing relentlessly towards the south, was the main danger and enemy; any power willing and able to give aid against Russia was a potential friend. Turkey's alliances have changed; their purpose has remained constant. After Prussia and Sweden, it was the turn of France and still more of Britain, who defended Turkey against Russia by force of arms in 1854-6, by threats or diplomacy in 1878 and on other occasions. Towards the end of the nineteenth century Britain and France were replaced as Turkey's allies by Germany, now regarded as the main bulwark against Russia. That alliance ended with the defeat of the Central Powers in 1918.

The revolutions in Russia and Anatolia on the one hand, and the Allied occupation of Istanbul on the other, created a new situation, in which a temporary coincidence of interests brought a temporary co-operation between the two revolutionary régimes. It ended when both of them overcame their enemies and gradually returned to what Atif Efendi would have called the 'permanent policies' of their two countries. Already at the Lausanne Conference in 1923, there was a chill in the relations between Russia, now firmly established in the Black Sea, and Turkey, now fully in control of Istanbul and the Straits. The Anglo-Turkish dispute over Mosul in 1924-5 brought a renewal of Turco-Soviet friendship, which however faltered under the impact of the Communist ideological offensive against Kemal and his régime in 1928-9. The capitalist depression and the Turkish adoption of *étatisme* brought some revival, which was further encouraged by a common mistrust of Italian fascist activities in Abyssinia and Spain.

That friendship came to an end in 1939, when the scanty reserve of goodwill built up during the period of revolutionary fraternity was finally dissipated by Soviet hectoring and demands. The ambiguities of Turkish policy during the war years were due largely to uncertainty as to which of the contending blocs was to be the bulwark of Turkey against Russian attack – to fulfil the role of Britain in 1854 and 1878, of

Germany in 1914. By 1947 it was apparent that that role had fallen to the United States. On March 12, President Truman announced a programme of military and economic aid to Turkey. Known as the Truman Doctrine, it marked the beginning of massive US involvement in the affairs of the Middle East.

At the time when the Napoleonic wars involved the Middle East for the first time in the European game of power politics and war, there was only one other independent state in the area – Persia. More remote from Europe than was the Ottoman Empire, her knowledge of European affairs was less direct, her reaction to them less sophisticated. Her problems, however, were not dissimilar. Persia, too, was threatened from the north, where the Russians had annexed several provinces and were penetrating others by both political and economic means. Like the Turks, the Persians looked to the West for guarantees – but were usually unable to get them. Germany was too far away to offer effective help; Britain fought shy of too close an involvement in Persian affairs. There were, moreover, many Persians who saw in the British Empire in India as great a danger to them as the Russian Empire to the north.

The guiding lines of Persian foreign policy were to seek support against Russia, or, failing that, to play the two neighbouring empires off against each other. They acquired great skill and at times won considerable success in this latter role, which the Romans called that of *tertius gaudens*, and which our time knows as positive neutralism. The Persian position in Asia was in some respects rather like that of the Poles in eastern Europe. As long as their two mighty neighbours differed, they could survive, and might even profit. If ever their two neighbours agreed, they were in danger of being submerged. This danger arose only once, at the time of the Anglo-Russian Entente of 1907. It was somewhat remote even then, and, apart from the uneasy Anglo-Russian co-operation during the two world wars, has not recurred.

The ending of British rule in India in 1947 removed one of the props on which Persian foreign policy had rested for a century and a half. In the place of the British Empire there were now two rival states in the Indian sub-continent, neither of them strong enough to constitute an effective counterpoise to Russia.

The power in the north remained, and Persian statesmen, alarmed by the Azerbaijan crisis of 1945-6, and the Soviet oil concession crisis of 1946-7, began to look for a new counterpoise. The announcement of the Truman Doctrine in 1947 showed them in what direction to look. Once before, in 1911, the Persians had turned to an American expert for advice and help against their two neighbours; in October 1947 they turned to America again for support against the one that remained. The agreement of October 6, providing for an American military mission and the purchase of American arms, was a first step. The next step, taken after some delays due to the Anglo-Persian oil crisis, was Persia's adherence to the Baghdad Pact in October, 1955.

At the beginning of the nineteenth century there were only two powers in the Middle East with the need for a foreign policy – Turkey and Persia. In the course of the century a third was added – Egypt. Under the rule of Muḥammad ʿAlī and his successors, Egypt, though not fully independent, acquired a considerable measure of autonomy – enough to permit the tentative emergence of an Egyptian foreign policy, or rather, of an Egyptian policy towards the other countries of the Middle East.

The problem was not a new one. As early as the ninth century, Egypt had become an independent centre of power within the Middle Eastern Islamic world, and a succession of dynasties ruling in Egypt had sketched and filled in the outlines of an Egyptian policy. The main principles of such a policy were summed up by the wazir Ibn Killis in the year 991, in his death-bed advice to the Fatimid Caliph al-ʿAzīz: keep the peace with the Byzantines as long as they keep it with you; be content with mention in the coinage and in public prayer by the Hamdanid amīrs of north Syria; do not spare the South Palestine Bedouin chief Mufarrij ibn al-Jarrāḥ if you get the chance.[41] Translated into more general and more modern terms, this would mean: keep on good terms with Europe as far as you can; be satisfied with a pliant but independent Syria; don't let go of the Gaza strip.

Palestine and Syria, lying beyond the most vulnerable of Egypt's four borders, have always been a prime concern of Egyptian governments, and the first area of Egyptian expansion. At the very least they sought to maintain a bridgehead in southern Palestine; if possible to extend Egypt authority to all Syria. Every independent Muslim ruler of Egypt, from Aḥmad b. Ṭūlūn to Saladin and from Muḥammad ʿAlī to President Nāṣir, has sooner or later taken the road to Damascus. Only the Mamluks, who ruled over a combined Syro-Egyptian empire for some two centuries, solved the Syrian problem. All the others ran into difficulties, encountered local resistance or external opposition, and were compelled to withdraw. Some of them lost Egypt as well as Syria in the process.

A new phase began with Muḥammad ʿAlī, a military commander, who made himself master of Egypt at the beginning of the nineteenth century. At home he tried to establish his régime economically by abolishing the old system of land-tenure and revenue-collection, concentrating the ownership of most land in his own hands, organizing state monopolies of trade, and building factories and industries under state auspices. Abroad, he established relations with a number of powers, and embarked on a series of military and political adventures in Arabia, the Sudan, Algeria, and above all Syria. Though most of these adventures failed, he succeeded in founding a new state, dynastic but also Egyptian, over which his descendants ruled until 1952.

Muḥammad ʿAlī was the first and also the last of his line to apply a really independent and comprehensive foreign policy. His successors were fully absorbed in their adventures in Africa, and in their complicated relations with the Ottoman suzerain and, later, the British occupying power. Their first independent venture in the Middle East was the intervention in Palestine in 1948. The resulting failure led directly to the fall of the dynasty and the emergence of a new régime. Its policies suggest some points of resemblance to those of Muḥammad ʿAlī, and other monarchs of a remoter past.

One other state in the Middle East has experience of diplomacy and foreign relations going back beyond the year 1918 – the Lebanon. The Republic of Lebanon in its present form is a modern creation. Mount Lebanon, however, has been the seat of autonomous Christian or Druze principalities for centuries. Already at the beginning of the seventeenth century the Druze prince Fakhr al-Dīn Maʿn created an independent Lebanon, and found a Western ally in the Grand Duke of Tuscany. After

Fakhr al-Dīn's fall and execution, the Shihāb princes of Lebanon managed to retain a large measure of autonomy. The Lebanese Maronites, by now the dominant community on the mountain, formed a relationship with France and with French and Italian religious orders that continued until modern times. During the communal disturbances of the nineteenth and the political rivalries of the twentieth century, some of the Maronite hierarchy and leaders developed the habit of looking to the West, and particularly to France, for support and protection. The tradition grew up of the Catholic bastion of Mount Lebanon – the brave and loyal support of Christian and Western civilization amid the hordes of Asia and Islam. During the period of the French Mandate, the French government relied very heavily on this little Catholic Ulster in the Islamic East. Though many Lebanese preferred the rival ideologies of Arab nationalism, many others, among the Maronites, accepted the role allotted to them, and leaned heavily in their policies on the French alliance.

The withdrawal of France from the Middle East thus created something of a crisis in Lebanese politics. The pressure of pan-Arabism inside the Lebanon became very powerful – more so indeed than in the neighbouring states, since the Lebanese Muslims, mistrusting the motives that had led to the creation of a separate Lebanon, were not bound to their country even by the same ties of sentiment as their co-religionists in Syria, Egypt, or Iraq. Among most of the Christians, many of the Shi'ites and Druzes, and some even of the Sunni Muslims, the sense of a separate Lebanese identity was, however, strong, and those of their leaders who believed that Lebanese survival depended on the West looked for a new guarantor to replace the vanished French. To many it seemed that the United States, the greatest power of the Christian West, with its own past record of cultural and educational work in the Lebanon, and its own current political, military, and economic interests in the area, was best fitted to take over the French role – as protector of the Christians and patron of the Lebanon. The policy of Lebanese separatism and Western alliance had always displeased the Arab nationalists; at a time of intense national and communal fervour and of violent anti-Western feeling, it enraged them to the point of civil war. In these circumstances, the United States soon showed that it was not prepared to accept the role that had been assigned to it, and the world was treated to the strange spectacle of an American military intervention, the purpose of which – if purpose may be judged by results – was to replace a pro-American government by another that was rather less pro-American and therefore more viable. As a means of simultaneously restoring peace and preventing the emergence of an anti-American government it worked well enough. The combination of viability with restrained hostility, in Middle Eastern régimes, was becoming a difficult and desirable objective of Western policy. It has remained so ever since. The encouragement or even the creation of régimes which have the merit of being only moderately anti-American has since then become, so it would seem, the principal aim of American policy in the Middle East.

The foreign policy of Israel is difficult to assess after so short a period of independent existence. Israel clearly has far less room for manoeuvre than any of her neighbours; she has to take account of the situation of the Jewish communities in other parts of the world, of the implacable enmity of the Arab states, of the generally unfriendly attitude of the Soviet Union, and of the terrible penalties for miscalculation – greater than for any other country in the world. The basic objective of Israeli foreign policy is survival – discussion turns only on how best to achieve this end. There is general agreement that this purpose is best served by a pro-Western policy, short of actual alliance.

Turkey and Persia are old sovereign states, with a habit of responsibility for their own survival and welfare. For them, national independence has been an accepted fact – an axiom of political life, in no need of assertion or demonstration. Though their independence has on occasion been threatened, it has never been lost, and their political thinking, with rare exceptions, has in consequence not been bedevilled by the problem of foreign rule and the struggle to end it. Their foreign policies, developed through practical experience over a long period, are directed towards the attainment of limited and definable national purposes, and are based on a normal mixture of tradition and calculation. These countries have grave internal problems, and Turkey has in recent years gone through violent political changes. It is remarkable, however, that these changes have had little discernible effect on Turkish foreign policy, which continues to be determined by the basic facts of Turkey's international position and predicament, rather than by the changing moods of internal politics.

In other words, in Turkey and, to a somewhat lesser extent, in Persia, foreign policy is formed and may be judged by the normal criteria of international relations in other parts of the world. Though these two countries together constitute a very substantial proportion of the area and population of the Middle East, they do not to any great extent share in its characteristic problems and attitudes, and do not usually receive much attention when these problems are discussed.

The Arab states are all comparatively new to independence, and their political *élites* have for long been dominated by the struggle to attain it. Now there are the problems of how to exercise it – a task involving a difficult readjustment of attitudes and ideas. It is not easy to turn from the vast and ill-defined aims of nationalist opposition, to the limited and practical calculations of national government; it is also difficult to accept the idea that complaints against repression and other evils must now be addressed to compatriots and co-religionists.

The foreign policies of the Arab states are concerned with three things – their relations with Israel, with one another, and with the outside world. On the first point they are agreed that Israel must be destroyed, though not on how this should be accomplished. The official Arab demand is no longer for the immediate destruction of Israel, but for its reduction to the frontiers laid down in the 1947 partition proposals – obviously as a first step towards its ultimate disappearance. Since Israel, clearly, would not submit voluntarily to such a truncation, and since the Arab states alone are unable to enforce it, this amounts in effect to a demand for an imposed settlement by the great powers – a kind of compulsory surgery on the conference table, in which, perhaps, Soviet arms would wield the knife, while Western diplomacy administered the anaesthetic. This was never a very likely contingency, and is less so now. Even if it were, one wonders whether the Arab states would really desire the restoration of great power control in the Middle East which the imposition of a solution – this or any other – would require.

The emergence of Israel in 1948 – or rather, the failure of the

Arab armies to prevent it, was a climactic event in the history of the Middle East, comparable in many ways with the landing of the Greeks in Izmir in 1919. It was bad enough to be dominated by the Franks – but they were after all the invincible masters of the world, who – on both occasions – had just defeated their enemies in a great war. It was a very different matter, and an intolerable humiliation, to submit to the Greeks or Jews – to local *dhimmis* whom the Muslims had long been accustomed to despise as inferiors. The Franks, moreover, would, sooner or later, go back whence they came. The Greek Great Idea – *megalē idea* – of a revived Byzantine empire, and the Zionist idea of a revived Jewish state, were clearly intended to be permanent. The same sense of outrage colours the Kemalist reaction against the Greeks, and the Arab reaction against Israel. Some of the difference in the subsequent development of Turkey and the Arab states may be ascribed to the fact that the Turks won their war, whereas the Arabs lost theirs.

During the thirties and early forties, the Arabs had been fed, by both the Axis and the Allies, on a diet of gross flattery which encouraged the tendency to self-adulation inherent in all nationalist movements. The military defeat in Palestine at the hands of the despised Jews was a terrible shock – hardly less than those of the earlier defeats which had led to the reforms and changes of the eighteenth and nineteenth centuries.

This time the pace was accelerated. Within a few years all the rulers that had sent their armies to defeat in Palestine had fallen – several of them by assassination. In March 1949 the Syrian Chief of Staff, Col Ḥusnī Zaʿīm, overthrew the Syrian government by a *coup d'état*, and established a military régime with himself as president. It was the first of a series of military revolutions and convulsions, which, with increasing violence, swept away the régimes of the kings, the pashas, and the conservative landowners, and unleashed new forces the nature and direction of which is still to be determined.

One of the most passionately asserted objectives of the new Arab movements is Arab unity, meaning at least close association, and at most the fusion of all the Arab states into one. There is general agreement on the need to follow the examples of Germany and Italy in nineteenth century Europe – but no agreement on which of the Arab states should play the role of

Prussia or Savoy. The rival candidates were for long Egypt and Iraq—and their rivalry, though sometimes interrupted, lasted a very long time, surviving several changes of régime in both countries. It was much complicated by the dealings of the great powers with both of them.

In 1945, when the war ended, Great Britain seemed firmly established as the dominant power in the Middle East, with overwhelming military force and political influence. The Arab League, so it seemed, was her instrument for the political integration of the region; the Middle East Supply Centre was its economic counterpart. Germany and Italy had been eliminated by defeat, France had been in effect evicted; America was not yet willing, Russia was not yet able, to play a role. Even the nationalist leaders were for the moment silent – anxiously aware of the might of the victors, and, for many, of their own suspect associations with the vanquished. It was not a moment to press demands.

Within ten years of the end of the war, the imposing structure of British power in the Middle East had been undermined, weakened, and destroyed; the British positions of strength, under attack from every side, were one by one abandoned or lost. The Middle East ceased to be an area of British predominance; it also ceased to be an area of predominantly Western influence.

A number of causes contributed to this contracting and withdrawal of British power. One of the first was the transfer of power in India, in 1947. It was as the paramount power in India that Britain first became actively involved in the affairs of the Middle East. The ending of that paramountcy greatly reduced both the need and the means for British action in the area. Another cause was the failure to solve the Palestine problem, and the abdication of the Palestine Mandate – a confession of weakness and irresolution which could not fail to stimulate and encourage further demands and attacks from every side. Some observers would add the inability of the makers of policy to recognize, understand and allow for the new forces which were arising in the Arab world and elsewhere, and which would sweep away the supports of British influence and power.

Underlying all these, and more fundamental than any of them, was the exhaustion of British power and resources after six years of war against mighty enemies. Already in March,

1947, President Truman had sought and obtained authority from Congress to give Greece and Turkey the help which they needed, and which Britain could no longer supply, in defending their independence and integrity against the Communist threat from the north. This policy was soon after extended to Persia. Towards the end of 1949 the US government was already considering a more active role in the Middle East as a whole. A meeting of US diplomats in the area was held in Istanbul in November, 1949, and was addressed by the Assistant Secretary of State, George C. McGhee. His remarks have been summarized by one of those present, the Ambassador to Israel, James G. McDonald:

'The basis of United States policy in the Middle East, McGhee told us, was to aid the development of all resources in the area, in order to lift the standard of living, and with an immediate two-fold purpose: (1) to avert the threat of Communism from the inside, and (2) to keep armed the defensible border states (Greece and Turkey) as a defence against any outside Soviet aggression.

'First and foremost, consequently, the United States could no longer take a back seat in the affairs of the Middle East. For, with the Communist threat mounting, Britain, hard-pressed by other problems, could no longer maintain full responsibility for the protection of Western interests and civilization in the area. The United States must shoulder an increasing part of the burden. In this respect, "complete agreement in principle" had been reached with Great Britain. Both countries, said McGhee, had the same general objectives, though in certain countries specific interests might not be identical. There were, he added, "points of asymmetry".

'It seemed to me', Mr McDonald continued, 'that this was an understatement of the extent of the divergence between our and British national interests.'[42]

During the years that followed, the divergencies – not so much between real national interests, as between the two manners of interpreting and defending them – became painfully obvious. In 1951 and 1952 British difficulties reached their climax; the murder of King 'Abdullah in Jordan; the oil crisis in Iran; the Anglo-Egyptian deadlock, followed by the Egyptian rejection of the four power proposal for a Middle East defence pact, and, soon after, the Anglo-Egyptian clash in the Canal Zone, culminating in the five-hour battle at Isma'ilia on January 25, 1952.

American policy in this period and the following seems to have been based on the belief that too close an association with Great Britain, too careful a regard for British interests, would tarnish the American image and obstruct American purposes. Britain, it was argued, even after her dramatic renunciation of empire in Asia and Africa, was still suspect in Asian and African eyes, not only as an ex-imperial power, but as one seeking to return. America, on the other hand, was herself an ex-colonial state – indeed, the first to win freedom by a successful revolution against British imperialism. Where America had led, others were following and would be bound to America by natural ties of sympathy and affinity.

The idea that the emergent nations of Asia and Africa would accept the American Revolution as the prototype of their own struggle against colonialism and spontaneously rally to American leadership was soon dissipated – by Indian policy during the Korean War, by Egyptian policy towards Russia, by Indonesia and Ghana and many others. It was never a very convincing idea, and rests on an analogy that is false to the point of absurdity. The American Revolution, after all, was made by Englishmen, concerned with the constitutional rights of Englishmen, not by Iroquois nationalists. It was not a victory against colonialism, but the ultimate triumph of colonialism – when the colonists have conquered and settled the colony so thoroughly that they are able to stand alone, without needing the further support of the mother country. It would be unfair and misleading to compare the American colonists of the eighteenth century with the white settler communities of today – but rather less absurd than to identify them with the white settlers' subjects.

It may seem unjust that America, which has never sought or held an inch of territory in the Middle East, should be accused of colonialism. But Middle Easterners are not wrong when they refuse to recognize America as something generically different from Europe, and untainted with the European past. For America is still part of that Romance and Germanic, Protestant and Catholic Western Christendom that is the historic West – the millennial adversary of the Islamic Empires, and the source of the devastating impact that has convulsed the Islamic world in modern times. Of this West, America is now the conscious leader, and she can no more renounce her association with it than with her language and her culture, her religions and her institutions.

As long as the illusion of such a renunciation persisted, it had a determining effect on American policies towards the Middle East and towards Britain and France; it had no discernible effect on the policies of the Middle Eastern states themselves.

The final stage in British withdrawal began in July, 1954 when, a few weeks after the conversations between Eisenhower and Churchill in Washington, an Anglo-Egyptian agreement was reached, providing for the evacuation by the British of the Suez Canal zone within twenty months. The last British troops were in fact withdrawn on April 2, 1955. It was obvious that the abandonment of the great Suez Canal base, for seventy years the keystone of the edifice of British power in the Middle East, would have immediate and far-reaching effects. Great expectations were placed in the agreement. At the time, the hope was widely entertained and still more widely expressed that, with the removal of the last Egyptian grievance against the West, real friendship and co-operation would at last become possible.

For those who held them, these hopes were swiftly disappointed. The general situation, far from getting better, got rapidly worse. The Egypt-Israel border, after a period of comparative calm, became once again the scene of new military clashes. The anticipated improvement in Egyptian relations with the West failed to come about. The liberation of their own soil left the Egyptians free to take up larger Arab and African causes; the attempt by the West to form a Middle Eastern alliance, and persuade Egypt to join it, provoked increasingly hostile reactions in Egypt, culminating in the signature in September, 1955 of an agreement with Czechoslovakia for the supply of arms. At one blow, the Soviet Union had established itself in a position of power and influence in the very heart of the Middle East.

In Turkey and Persia American aid was welcomed, and American leadership accepted. Neither of these was an ex-colonial country; for them America was not the ancient pioneer of anti-colonialism, but the new leader of the West, and as such their natural defender against the old and familiar threat from Russia. In the Arab countries there was no such awareness, based on experience, of Russian expansionism, and therefore no such desire to seek or accept Western – American or other – support. Only one Arab country – Iraq – actually entered the pact. It was taken in by an unpopular and unrepresentative régime, which had not long to survive. There can be little doubt that its pro-Western alignment was one of the main causes of its overthrow. In the light of what we now know of Nūrī al-Saʿīd's secret approaches to the Germans in 1940, we may wonder how effective the alliance would have been if the régime had survived and been put to the test.

Whatever its apparent military advantages, the attempt to involve Iraq in a Western defensive system can now be seen as a major political error. In other Arab lands it aroused bitter hostility, and led directly to negotiations with the Communist bloc, the way for which was prepared by Colonel Nāṣir's participation in the neutralist conference at Bandoeng in April, 1955 – his first introduction to international, as distinct from Middle Eastern politics. It was a portentous beginning.

The interest of the Soviet Union in the Middle East was not new. At the meeting between Hitler and Molotov in November, 1940, the Soviet government, according to the captured German documents, demanded German agreement to a Soviet military and naval base on the Bosphorus and the Dardanelles, and recognition of 'the area south of Batum and Baku in the general direction of the Persian Gulf ... as the center of the aspirations of the Soviet Union'.[43]

After the German attack on Russia these plans were shelved. They reappeared at the end of the war, when circumstances seemed favourable for their fulfilment, with Persia under occupation, Turkey isolated by her protracted neutrality, and Russia part of the victorious alliance. On that occasion the attempt failed; the communist republic set up in Persian Azerbaijan was overthrown, and the demand for bases in the Turkish straits steadfastly refused. Apart from the abortive agreement with Dr Mosaddegh in Persia in 1953, the Soviets made no further attempt to intervene at government level in Middle Eastern affairs, but preferred to stay on the sidelines, waiting for the 'inevitable contradictions of capitalism' to disrupt the political and economic structure of the Middle East, and thus prepare the way for communism. Where convenient, the working of these contradictions was aided by what one might call routine subversion.

The return of Russia in 1955 to an active role in Middle Eastern politics was not – or should not have been – in itself surprising. The timing was masterly. The Arab states were divided and angry about the pro-Western alignment of Iraq; Egypt was bitterly hostile, and had just received a flattering initiation into the society of the great Asian neutralists. Arab-Israel relations were more than usually bad, and continued to distort political thinking in the region generally. The British Middle Eastern base at Suez was being dismantled, and transferred to Cyprus, which in turn was convulsed by a fierce conflict. This again had embroiled Turkey and Greece, on whose friendship and goodwill the south-eastern corner of NATO so largely depended.

The Soviet move seems to have begun in April, when *Izvestya* published a Foreign Ministry statement deploring 'the recent deterioration in the situation' and expressing the intention of the USSR to develop closer relations with the countries of the Middle East. During the spring and summer there were intensive diplomatic activities, including exchanges of visits and missions with several Arab countries. Attempts to ignore and then play down reports of an arms deal between Egypt and the Soviet bloc were abandoned at the end of September, when news of the agreement was officially released.

Far more striking – and alarming – than the arms deal itself was the wave of almost ecstatic joy with which it was received all over the Arab world. The Syrian, Lebanese and Jordanian chambers of deputies at once voted resolutions of congratulation to Colonel Nāṣir, and almost the entire Arab press greeted the news with rapturous acclamation. Even Nūrī al-Saʿīd felt constrained to send a message of congratulation and approval to the Egyptian leader.

This response was not due to any special love of Russia, nor to any desire to see either communism or Soviet power extended in the Middle East; it was due rather to a lively appreciation of the quality of Colonel Nāṣir's act as a slap in the face for the West. The Colonel's slap, and the red-faced, agitated and ineffectual Western response to it, gave a dramatic and satisfying expression to a mood and wish that united many if not most Arabs – the mood of revulsion from the West, and the wish to spite and humiliate it. 'Most Westerners', says Professor Cantwell Smith, 'have simply no inkling of how deep and fierce is the hate, especially of the West, that has gripped the modernizing Arab.'⁴⁴

There were statesmen and even governments in the Arab world who believed in a policy of co-operation or association with the West. They could, however, pursue such a policy only by disregarding, misleading, or suppressing popular feeling – and did so at peril of their lives. Until very recently, on the other hand, the acceptance of Russian favours carried no such risks to personal safety or political popularity, and even now is far less suspect than any leaning towards the West. The same double standard towards the Soviets and the West could be seen in many things – in the silent, almost surreptitious pocketing of Western gifts, and the loud welcoming of Russian benefactions; in the quiet acceptance of Russian chiding, and the angry riposte to the mildest Western comments; in the ceaseless harrying of the last retreating rearguards of Western empire, while Russian rule over vast Muslim territories in Asia passes uncriticized, almost unnoticed. Despite some recent improvement, the prevailing attitude to the West is one of deep mistrust and hostility. Collaboration with the West still needs to be excused or, better still, concealed. Collaboration with Russia does not, even among anti-Communist nationalists. From time to time the West has found – or procured – régimes that are willing to collaborate with it, if only in secret and within narrow limits. The difficulty is that such collaboration is always uncertain, and the régimes that provide it either untrustworthy or insecure – sometimes both.

Why is this so, and what can we do about it? There is no lack of answers to these questions, in the form of specific problems and varying solutions to them. Some speak wistfully of how easy all would be if only Arab wishes could be met – this being usually interpreted to mean those wishes that can be satisfied at the expense of other parties. This kind of policy, called appeasement by its opponents, has many variants, most of which can be reduced to a formula on these lines: 'If only the others would give way, *we* and the Arabs could get on perfectly well.

Let *us* therefore induce the *others* to meet Arab demands.' The identity of 'we' and 'the others' can be filled in according to taste; nationally – America, Britain, France, Israel; or sectionally – politicians, generals, businessmen, professors; – or in whatever other ways interest and prejudice may indicate.

A version of this formula, current for a time in some American circles, was that were it not for the unfortunate and adventitious association with West European imperialism and with Zionism, there could be an idyllic marriage of American interests and Arab nationalism, in which the latter would be firm and independent against all others but gracefully acquiescent in American requirements. In that happy day there would be bases for the military, treaties for the diplomats, concessions for the businessmen and converts for the missionaries, with a general glow of mutual friendship and goodwill. It is a pretty picture – but of an apocalyptic rather than an historical quality. The United States appears well satisfied with considerably less.

Most Arabs would put Zionism and imperialism in the first place as the reasons for their hostility to the West. Both are indeed deeply and sincerely hated – yet neither provides a satisfying explanation of the Arab mood and malaise. The votes of the Soviet bloc helped to carry the famous United Nations resolution under which Israel was established; the *de jure* recognition of the Soviet Union was accorded to Israel on the day of its birth; arms from Czechoslovakia saved the new state from strangulation in its infancy – yet all this left no noticeable residue of resentment or ill-will against Russia. In any case, the problem is wider than the Arab lands and their specific concerns. There are many states in Asia and Africa which are unconcerned with the Palestine problem, which even maintain friendly relations with Israel, but which apply the same double standard in their dealings with Russia and the West.

Is the problem, then, one of imperialism, of which Zionism, in Arab eyes, is one particular manifestation? This certainly brings us nearer to the root of the matter, for the hatred of imperialism is undoubtedly one of the most powerful forces in the Arab world today. But in that case, why should this hatred include America, which has never ruled any part of the Middle East, and exclude Russia, which still rules – not always gently – in such ancient Muslim, Asian cities as Samarkand and

Bukhara, and many others besides? The same question may be asked in many Asian and African lands, beyond the Arab world.

We shall be better able to understand this situation if we view the present discontents of the Middle East not as a conflict between states or nations, but as a clash between civilizations. The 'Great Debate', as Gibbon called it, between Christendom and Islam has been going on, in one form or another, since the Middle Ages. For the past century and a half Islam has been subject to the domination of the West, a domination that has posed to the Muslim peoples, and continues to pose even after political control has ended, tremendous problems of readjustment – political, social, economic, cultural, psychological – both in their dealings with others, and in their own internal affairs. Even after liberation, the intelligent and sensitive Arab cannot but be aware of the continued subordination of his culture to that of the West. His richest resource is oil – but it is found and extracted by Western processes and machines, to serve the needs of Western inventions. His greatest pride is his new army – but it uses Western arms, wears Western-style uniforms, and marches to Western tunes. His ideas and ideologies, even of anti-Western revolt, derive ultimately from Western thought. His knowledge even of his own history and culture owes much to Western scholarship. His writers, his artists, his architects, his technicians, even his tailors, testify by their work to the continued supremacy of Western civilization —the ancient rival, once the pupil, now the model, of the Muslim.* Even the gadgets and garments, the tools and amenities of his everyday life are symbols of bondage to an alien and dominant culture, which he hates and admires, imitates but cannot share. It is a deeply wounding, deeply humiliating experience.

In the twilight world of popular myths and images, the West is the source of all evil – and the West is a single whole, the parochial sub-divisions of which are hardly more important to the average Middle Easterner than are those of the Middle East for the average Westerner. Old sovereign states like Turkey and Persia have developed consistent foreign policies based on national interests and rational calculations; Arab policies are

---

* Even Russia, the alternative model, is in many respects an earlier and more successful imitator of the West.

still at the mercy of a mood of ethnic and communal collectivism, which treats the West as a collective enemy.

The Russians succeeded where the Americans had failed, in presenting themselves to the Arabs as something generically different from the West. They succeeded because they *are* something generically different, while America is not. America is inescapably part of the West, of which she has now become the leader. Russia is not part of the West, but on the contrary is opposed to the West – in ideology, economics, and politics, in way of life and in international affairs. For this reason alone she can command sympathy and support, as did the Nazis a generation ago – often from the same persons. Even at the present time the memory of Hitler is responsible for a good deal of pro-German feeling, which worthy visitors from the West German Federal Republic find commercially convenient but morally embarrassing. In the main, those who once turned to Berlin now turn to Moscow, as the new citadel of anti-Western power. Russian colonialism was in areas remote from the Arab lands, and in forms unfamiliar to the Arab peoples, who knew only the maritime, liberal, commercial empires of the West. It has, therefore, to a large extent escaped notice. Even where it is intellectually apprehended, it has no emotional impact on them comparable with that of the Western kind which they have personally experienced. This deficiency the Russians are now making good, with true Soviet tempo. An interesting criticism of the Russians, occasionally heard of late, is that they are just like the Americans – another lot of Europeans in disguise – another extension of the historic West.

The impact of the West in the Arab lands has created real problems, through the economic, social, and political dislocations to which it gave rise, and the cultural inferiority complex which it engendered. These are in the long run far more important than the various specific political issues as a source of discontent and resentment. They are not, however, easy to formulate and discuss on a political level, especially in countries which have no tradition of such discussion; nor can the blame for them readily be thrown on nameable and recognizable culprits. It is, therefore, the surface political issues that are most to the fore, both as a focus and as a manifestation of anti-Western feeling. It is not always easy to tell whether one or other of these issues is an irritant or an outlet – a cause of tension, or a relatively harmless way of releasing it. The events of the last few years seem to show that as the successive veils of political distraction are stripped away, the tension becomes greater and not less.

It is no doubt with these considerations in mind – disbelief in the possibility or efficacy of real appeasement – that some have recommended the contrary policy, of firmly opposing, or at least disregarding, Arab nationalism. This line is often supported by such dubious pieces of colonial folklore as 'the Arab only understands force'. The Arab does of course understand force, and may at times be convinced by it. But it is not the only thing he understands. An extreme form of this policy was the ill-fated Anglo-French expedition to Suez in 1956; others include the brusque rejection by Mr Dulles, in July of the same year, of the Egyptian request for help in the Aswan dam project, and the cool indifference of French policy in the Arab east during the Algerian war. Another variant is the imposition or maintenance of pro-Western régimes regardless of popular sentiment.

Apart from the moral aspects, one may question whether such a policy, of force or manipulation, is either feasible or desirable, and wonder about its probable effects in Asia and Africa – indeed also in Europe and America. But is there really only a straight choice between domination and appeasement? Must we persist in regarding the Arabs as spoilt children, who must either be smacked and locked in the nursery, or else stuffed with cream cakes to keep them quiet? Is there no way of achieving a rational and normal relationship, based on a realistic assessment of the interests, needs and circumstances of both sides?

The crisis in the Middle East, it has been suggested, arises not from a quarrel between states but from a clash between civilizations. Civilizations can have no foreign policy, but governments must, and in the Middle East the West faces urgent problems. The argument is often heard that we must, in some way, come to terms with Arab nationalism.

Here I propose to set forth, in a series of propositions, what seem to me to be the essential features of the present situation in the Arab lands, and the considerations that should determine the formulation of a Western policy towards them.

Since 1955 the Middle East has ceased to be an area of

exclusively Western influence. It is not likely to become so again.

By revulsion from more than a century and a half of Western influence and domination, by reaction against Western leadership in every significant field of human endeavour, the Arab attitude to the West is now generally hostile. In contrast, the Arab attitude to Russia, not coloured by any previous record of relations, has been emotionally neutral.

This being so, in any struggle for positions of power and influence, with Russia and the West using the same political and economic means, Russia has a great initial psychological advantage.

This advantage is reinforced by the familiar and intelligible authoritarian methods and political style of the Russians, as contrasted with the unfamiliar and, to most Arabs, unintelligible democratic processes of the West.

As the Russians become involved in the Middle East, they are losing their initial advantages, and are encountering some of the suspicions, resentments and frustrations familiar to their Western predecessors and counterparts. The interests of the West do not absolutely require the interruption of this process of reciprocal education.

The Arab countries are going through a profound crisis in their history, causing a period of economic, social, and political instability. This crisis, though it may be exploited by communists, is not caused by them.

In Arab eyes, this crisis is caused by the West. This is partially true, in that its origins may be traced back to the disruptive effects of westernization on traditional Islamic society. Though the transformation was due at least as much to Muslim westernizers as to Western overlords, the crisis of Arab society was precipitated by a movement of recognizably Western provenance. The resulting sense of outrage colours Arab attitudes to the West, and to any project or proposal emanating from it. Contributory causes of hostility are the conflict with Israel and the continuance of Western influence in some parts of the Arab world.

There are signs that the crisis of anti-Western hostility may be passing its peak. Special care is needed not to provoke a relapse.

British policy failed in the Middle East when British weakness and lack of support were revealed. The power and wealth of the United States, however, still command respect, and will win some initial success even for misguided policies; they cannot in the nature of things obtain the kind of deference which is given to those who use their power more ruthlessly.[45]

A natural and healthy solution to the Arab crisis can be found only by the Arabs themselves. Outside interference, from East or West, delays such a solution, by diverting Arab attention to political problems and adventures, and thus impeding the emergence of constructive Arab statesmanship.

To the achievement of such a solution the West can perhaps make a contribution – its only possible constructive contribution – by giving economic and technical aid, provided that some means can be found of reconciling the giver's interest in the economic and efficient use of his gift, and the taker's interest in avoiding any infringement of his independence and freedom of action. Such aid should be given for economic and social development, not for political and military adventures. Its objective should be the long-term improvement of the economic and, therefore, ultimately, the political conditions of the Arab countries, not the buttressing of particular Arab régimes or policies. The most that can be hoped for by way of reward is a reluctance to provoke those who confer such benefits to the point of withholding them – that is, of course, until they are no longer required. Any hope of political or military support for the West in return for such aid would be illusory, and any attempt to secure it self-defeating, though some lesser tokens of appreciation might not unreasonably be claimed.

Israel is now eighteen years old and generally recognized, and its continued existence, like that of any other sovereign state, has become an axiom of the present system of world politics. Some Arabs, however reluctantly, are beginning to accept this. Though no general solution of the problem of Arab-Israel relations is in sight, it would be brought nearer if the problem could be disengaged from the conflicts of the great powers.

As a necessary preliminary to the solution of the Arab crisis, the interests of the Arabs require the political neutralization of their countries. This should mean genuine neutrality, and not a policy of exacerbating and exploiting the rivalries of the great powers for political or other advantage.

In view of the Western handicap in the Arab lands, the West's interest lies in the cessation of the cold war in that area. The West's interests thus coincide with the real interests of the Arabs, though not necessarily with the policies of particular Arab governments.

Even the Soviet Union may find some advantage in limiting the scope and range of conflict in an area which, in its internal political style and international political role, so disquietingly resembles the Balkan peninsula in the early twentieth century, the scene of many reverses to Russian policies and interests.

Coming to terms with Arab nationalism would be a good thing, if it were possible. It cannot be achieved, with any permanency, by coming to terms with individual nationalist leaders, who, by the very act of coming to terms, are in danger of losing their following. It is difficult to obtain precise terms from a movement which represents a mood more than a programme.

Neither total repression of Arab opposition nor total appeasement of Arab demands is possible. The partial or sectional use of either method is unlikely to advance Western interests in the Arab world.

As long as the cold war continues, the West must safeguard certain minimum positions in and near the Arab world, in self defence. These should be kept to the absolute minimum possible and, on an agreed definition, should be treated as the combined interests of the Western alliance.

Apart from this, the West should ostentatiously disengage from Arab politics, and in particular from inter-Arab politics. While bound by both honour and self-interest to assist those who have put their trust in the West, it should seek or manufacture no further Arab allies, and neither court nor rebuff Arab governments. This need not harm and might help normal commercial relations, which on the whole are more important to the Arabs than to the West.

After a period of time, better relations between the West and the Arab world may – probably will – become possible. Friendship will be possible only when Arab nationalism is prepared to come to terms with the West.

NOTES TO CHAPTERS

CHAPTER ONE

1. A. T. Mahan, 'The Persian Gulf and International Relations', in *National Review*, September 1902 (reprinted in *idem, Retrospect and Prospect*, London 1903); V. Chirol, *The Middle Eastern Question*, London 1903. See further R. H. Davison, 'Where is the Middle East?' in *Foreign Affairs*, July 1960, 665-75, and B. Lewis and P. M. Holt (editors), *Historians of the Middle East*, London 1962, 1-3, where some of these points are discussed.

CHAPTER TWO

2. See for example R. F. Kreutel and O. Spies, *Leben und Abenteuer des Dolmetschers Osman Aga*, Bonn 1954, 171; Yirmi Sekiz Mehmed Efendi, *Paris Sefaretnamesi*, Istanbul 1302, 99 (on the gardens of the Trianon).

3. Asim, *Tarih*, Istanbul n.d., i, 376; cited in B. Lewis. 'The Impact of the French Revolution on Turkey', in *Journal of World History*, i (1953), 118.

4. A. Adnan [Adîvar], *La science chez les Turcs ottomans*, Paris 1939, 57.

5. Muḥammad Iqbāl, *Peyām-i Mashriq*, Lahore, n.d. 255. French translation by Eva Meyerovitch and Mohammad Achena, *Message de l'Orient*, Paris 1956, 189.

CHAPTER THREE

6. Sadullah Pasha, *1878 Paris Ekspozisiyonu*, in Ebüzziya Tevfik, *Nümune-i Edebiyat-i Osmaniye*, (1st ed. Istanbul 1296) 3rd ed. 1306, 288. In this, Sadullah Pasha is echoing an old dictum, recorded by the ninth century Arabic author Ibn Qutayba, and repeated by many subsequent Islamic authors, that 'There is no rule without soldiers, no soldiers without money, no money without prosperity, no prosperity without justice and good government'. The change in the text is significant. (Ibn Qutayba, '*Uyūn al-Akhbār*, ed. Carl Brockelmann, i, Berlin 1900, 26; cf. A. K. S. Lambton, 'Justice in the medieval Persian theory of kingship', in *Studia Islamica*, xvii, 1962, 100).

7. W. G. Browne, *Travels in Africa, Egypt, and Syria from the year 1792 to 1798*, London 1806, 432-3.

8. Lutfi, *Tarih*, viii, Istanbul 1328, 15; B. Lewis, *The Emergence of Modern Turkey*, London 1961, 110.

9. Shaykh Rifā'a Rāfi' al-Taḥṭāwī, *Takhlīṣ al-Ibrīz fī Talkhīṣ Bārīz*, (1st ed. Bulaq 1265) ed. Mahdī 'Allām, Aḥmad Badawī and Anwar Lūqā, Cairo n.d. [?1958], 150.

10. Sadîk Rifat Pasha, *Müntahabat-i Âsâr*, Istanbul n.d. Cf. Ş. Mardin, *The Genesis of Young Ottoman Thought*, Princeton 1962, 169 ff., and B. Lewis, *Emergence*, 129 ff.

11. Dufferin to Granville, 6 Feb. 1883, *Parliamentary Papers*, c. 3529, Egypt no. 6, 1883, lxxxiii, 43.

12. T. E. Lawrence, *The Seven Pillars of Wisdom*, chapter III.

13. Cited in Malcolm H. Kerr, 'The Emergence of a Socialist Ideology in Egypt', in *Middle East Journal*, xvi (1962), 142-3.

14. In *Al-Ahrām*, August 4 1961. French translation in *Orient*, v/19 (1961) 151-8.

15. B. Berenson, *Aesthetics and History*, (1st ed. 1948) repr. N.Y. 1954.

16. Interview with R. K. Karanjia on September 28, 1958, reported in *Al-Ahram* September 29, 1958; English translation in *President Gamal Abdel Nasser's Speeches and Press-Interviews 1958*, Cairo [?1959], 402. The *Protocols* were also featured in an article by Ṣalāḥ Dasūqī, in the official Egyptian cultural journal *Al-Majalla*, iv, no. 47, Nov. 1960, 7-11; cf. ibid, v, no. 49, Jan. 1961, 134-6. On war-time collaboration with the Axis, see for example Anwar El Sadat, *Revolt on the Nile*, London 1957, 34 ff.

CHAPTER FOUR

16a. There is still much confusion in the use of the two terms. The loyalty of a plural society such as India, for example, might better be described as patriotic rather than nationalistic, despite the common use of the latter term. Patriotism helped to create modern India. Nationalism could well disrupt and destroy it.

17. Al-Jurjānī, *Ta'rifāt*, Istanbul 1327, 171; al-Jāḥiẓ, *Al-Ḥanīn ilā'l-awṭān*, ed. Shaykh Ṭāhir al-Jazā'irī, Cairo 1333; German translation in [O. Rescher], *Excerpte und Übersetzungen aus den Schriften des Philologen und Dogmatikers Gâḥiẓ aus Baçra* ... i, Stuttgart 1931, 488-97. Ibn Shaddād, *Al-A'lāq al-Khaṭīra* ... ed. D. Sourdel, i/I, Damascus 1953, 2 ff. Other examples in G. E. von Grunebaum, 'The Response to Nature in Arabic Poetry', in *Journal of Near Eastern Studies*, iv (1943) 144-6.

18. Ali Sher Navoy, *Khamsa*, Tashkent 1960, 750. My thanks are due to Dr. Gandjei for this reference.

19. Ahmed Refik (ed), 'Ali Efendinin Sefaretnamesi ...' in

Tarih-i Osmani Encümeni Mecmuasî, (1329), 1459; Lewis, *Emergence,* 329.

20. Lewis, *Emergence,* 329-40; Mardin, *Genesis,* 210, 326 f, etc.
21. Mustafa Nihat Özön, *Namîk Kemal ve Ibret Gazetesi,* Istanbul 1938, 81 ff.; cf. Mardin 327, Lewis, *Emergence,* 330 ff.
22. Sir Lewis Namier, *Vanished Supremacies,* (1st ed. 1958), London 1962, 49, 50.
23. Cited by Namier, *op. cit.,* 62, 63.
24. U. Heyd, *Foundations of Turkish nationalism,* London 1950, 43; Lewis, *Emergence,* 345.
25. Al-Tha'ālibī, *Fiqh al-Lugha,* Cairo 1284, 3; cited by 'A. 'A. al-Dūrī, *Al-Judhūr al-ta'rīkhiyya li'l-qawmiyya al-'Arabiyya,* Beirut, 1960, 46.
26. I owe this observation to Prof. M. Berger.
27. Midhat Cemal Kuntay, *Sarîklî Ihtilâlcî Ali Suavi,* Istanbul 1946, 59; Mardin, *Genesis,* 372.
27a Özön 263-5, 81; Mardin 327-8; Lewis 332-3.
28. Mehmet Akif [Ersoy], *Hakkîn sesleri,* 1913, in *Safahat,* 6th ed. Istanbul 1963, 205-6.

CHAPTER FIVE

29. M. Plessner, 'Ist der Zionismus gescheitert?' in *Mitteilungsblatt* (Wiener Library, London), October 24, 1952, no. 42.
30. Cited by A. Bausani, 'Note su Shah Walīullāh di Delhi (1703-1762)', in *Annali dell'Istituto Universitario Orientale di Napoli,* n.s. x (1961) 99.
31. Özön 33, cited in Lewis, *Emergence,* 335.
32. *Al-'Urwa al-Wuthqā,* Cairo 1957, 10; cited in P. J. Vatikiotis, 'Muhammad 'Abduh and the quest for a Muslim humanism', in *Arabica,* IV (1957), 62.
33. Muhammad al-Bahay, *Al-Fikr al-Islāmī al-hadīth wa-silatuhu bi'l-isti'mār al-gharbī,* Cairo 1957.
34. Liman von Sanders, *Fünf Jahre Türkei,* Berlin 1920, 330-1; English translation, *Five Years in Turkey,* Annapolis 1928, 212.
35. Cited in Mahmud Kemal Inal, *Osmanlî devrinde son Sadrîazamlar,* Istanbul 1940-53, 1892; translated in Lewis, *Emergence,* 352.
36. Cited in P. Rondot, *L'Islam et les musulmans d'aujourd'hui,* i, Paris 1958, 253.
37. W. Cantwell Smith, *Islam in Modern History,* Princeton 1957, 156-7.
38. Nabih Amin Faris, 'The Islamic Community and Communism', in W. Z. Laqueur (ed), *The Middle East in Transition,* London 1958. 353, n.3.

39. Jevdet, *Tarih*, v, Istanbul 1309, 12. My thanks are due to Dr T. Naff for drawing my attention to this episode.
40. Jevdet, vi, 400-1.
41. The testament of Ibn Killis is reported by several Arabic historians, e.g. Ibn al-Qalānisī, *Dhayl Taʿrīkh Dimashq*, ed. Amedroz, Leiden 1908, 32; Ibn al-Jawzī, *Al-Muntaẓam*, vii, Hyderabad 1358, 156; Ibn Khallikān, *Wafayāt al-Aʿyān*, Bulaq 1299,ii, 442 (English translation by M. G. De Slane, *Biographical Dictionary*, Paris-London 1843-71, iv. 365); Miskawayh, *The Eclipse of the Abbasid Caliphate*, ed. and tr. Amedroz and Margoliouth Oxford 1920 iii, 185, tr. ii, 398; variant versions in Ibn al-Athīr, *Kāmil*, ed. Tornberg, Leiden, ix, 54, and Maqrīzī, *Khiṭaṭ*, Bulaq 1270, ii, 7. See also W. J. Fischel, *Jews in the Economic and Political Life of Mediaeval Islam*, London 1937, 60, n. 1.
42. J. G. McDonald, *My Mission in Israel 1948-1951*, London 1951, 181-2.
43. U.S. Department of State, *Nazi-Soviet Relations, 1939-1941. Documents from the Archives of the German Foreign Office*, ed. R. J. Sontag and J. S. Beddie. Dept. of State publication 3023, Washington 1948, 259; cf. ibid 244-5 and 270.
44. Cantwell Smith, *Islam*, 159.
45. Thus, for example, a broadcast in the 'Voice of the Arab Nation' programme, transmitted from Cairo in Arabic on March 19, 1963, at 10 a.m. GMT, called on the 'free officers, soldiers, students and Arab brothers' in Saudi Arabia and Jordan to overthrow their rulers, 'the lackeys who have sold their honour and dignity and who co-operate with the arch-enemies of the Arabs – the English, the Americans and the Jews.' In contrast, even the strongly anti-Communist government that followed Qāsim in Iraq was careful to disclaim any hostility to the Russians or the Soviet Union.

SUGGESTIONS FOR FURTHER READING

GENERAL

A definition of the Middle East, with some notes on the history and usage of the term, was attempted by R. H. Davison ('Where is the Middle East?' in *Foreign Affairs*, July 1960, pp. 665–75; reprinted in R. H. Nolte, ed., *The modern Middle East*, New York 1963). Among numerous general surveys and reference books on the area, mention may be made of those published by the Royal Institute of International Affairs (*The Middle East, a political and economic survey*, 3rd ed. London 1958) and by Europa publications (*The Middle East and North Africa: a survey and directory of the countries of the Middle East*, 12th ed. London 1965). Much relevant information will also be found in the French survey of the Muslim world edited by Louis Massignon (*Annuaire du monde musulman: statistique, historique social et économique*, 4th ed. Paris 1955). The geography of the region has been treated by W. B. Fisher (*The Middle East: a physical, social and regional geography*, 3rd ed. London 1956); S. H. Longrigg (*The Middle East: a social geography*, London 1963), and, earlier, by D. G. Hogarth (*The nearer East*, London 1902). The religious and social geography of the Islamic lands and peoples has been examined by Xavier de Planhol (*The World of Islam*, Ithaca N.Y. 1959).

Detailed studies on the life of the peasants and of the nomads have been written by J. Weulersse (*Paysans de Syrie et du Proche Orient*, Paris [1946], and by R. Montagne (*La civilisation du desert: nomades d'Orient et d'Afrique*, Paris 1947). Aspects of Turkish and Persian society have been studied by P. Stirling (*Turkish village*, London 1965); Ann K. S. Lambton (*Landlord and peasant in Persia*, London 1953, and, on a broader theme, *Islamic society in Persia*, London 1954); and Arab society by G. Baer (*Population and society in the Arab East*, London 1964), and in the volume edited by S. N. Fisher (*Social forces in the Middle East*, Ithaca N.Y. 1955). Other presentations by social scientists include the work of an anthropologist (Carleton S. Coon, *Caravan: the story of the Middle East*, New York 1951) and two books by sociologists, one American (Morroe Berger, *The Arab world today*, London 1962) and the other French (J.

Berque, *The Arabs: their history and future,* London 1964).
Short historical introductions are available on the Arabs (B.
Lewis, *The Arabs in history,* revised ed. London 1965; F.
Gabrieli, *The Arabs: a compact history,* New York 1963; P. K.
Hitti, *The Arabs: a short history,* London 1948; A. Hottinger,
The Arabs: their history, culture and place in the modern world,
London 1963; F. Gabrieli, *The Arab revival,* London 1961; P. M.
Holt, *Egypt and the Fertile Crescent 1516–1922,* London 1966)
and on the Persians (Sir Arnold T. Wilson, *Persia,* London 1932;
R. N. Frye, *Iran,* 2nd ed. London 1960; A. Bausani, *I Persiani,*
Florence 1962; V. Minorsky, 'Storia dell' Iran islamico', in *Le
civiltà dell' Oriente,* i, Rome 1956, pp. 461–513). In the absence
of any modern outline of Turkish history, the reader must still
have recourse to earlier works by Sir Edward Creasy (*A history
of the Ottoman Turks,* revised ed., London 1877, reprinted
Beirut 1962) and S. Lane-Poole (*Turkey,* London 1888), supple-
mented by brief but more modern accounts in standard works of
reference, such as the *Encyclopaedia of Islam* (art. 'Turks' in
first ed., by J. H. Kramers), *Historia Mundi* (vol. vii, Berne
1957, chapter on 'Das osmanische Reich' by A. Bombaci pp.
439–85), *Le civiltà dell' Oriente* (vol. i, chapter on the Turks,
by Ettore Rossi, pp. 515–82) and the *Handbuch der Orientalistik*
(vol. vi, Leiden-Cologne 1959, chapters on the Ottoman Empire
by H. F. Kissling, H. Scheel and G. Jaeschke, pp. 3–97). Works
on the modern history of Iran and Turkey include those of P.
Avery (*Modern Iran,* London 1965); B. Lewis (*The emergence
of modern Turkey,* revised imp., London 1965); G. Lewis (*Turkey,* revised ed., London 1965). Some of the general problems of
modern Arab history are discussed by P. M. Holt (*The study
of modern Arab history,* London 1965) and F. Gabrieli ('La
storia moderna dei popoli arabi', in *Atti del X Congresso Inter-
nazionale di Science storiche,* v, Rome 1955, pp. 273–301). Works
on the modern history of individual countries include: Egypt
(M. Rifaat Bey, *The awakening of modern Egypt,* London 1947;
A. Hasenclever, *Geschichte Aegyptens im 19 Jahrhundert,* Halle
1917; G. Young, *Egypt,* London 1927; M. Colombe, *L'Evolution
de l'Egypte 1924–1950,* Paris 1951); Syria and Lebanon (H.
Lammens, *La Syrie: Précis historique,* 2 vols., Beirut 1921; P. K.
Hitti, *History of Syria,* London 1951; idem, *Lebanon in history,*
London 1957; Z. N. Zeine, *The struggle for Arab independence:
Western diplomacy and the rise and fall of Faisal's kingdom in
Syria,* Beirut 1960; N. A. Ziadeh, *Syria and Lebanon,* London
1957; S. H. Longrigg, *Syria and Lebanon under French Mandate,*

London 1958; K. S. Salibi, *The modern history of Lebanon,* London 1965); Iraq (S. H. Longrigg, *Four centuries of modern Iraq,* Oxford 1925; idem, *Iraq 1900–1950,* London 1953); Arabia (H. St. J. Philby, *Saudi Arabia,* London 1955; J. B. Kelly, *Eastern Arabian frontiers,* London 1964; R. Bayly Winder, *Saudi Arabia in the 19th century,* London 1966); Sudan (P. M. Holt, *A modern history of the Sudan,* 2nd ed., London 1963); Russian Empire and Soviet Union (G. Wheeler, *The modern history of Soviet Central Asia,* London 1964; Mary Holdsworth, *Turkestan in the 19th century,* London 1959; D. M. Lang, *A modern history of Georgia,* London 1962). The economic history of the Middle East has so far received little attention. General introductions have been provided by Z. Y. Hershlag (*Introduction to the modern economic history of the Middle East,* Leiden 1964) and in a collection of papers and documents edited by C. Issawi (*The economic history of the Middle East, 1800–1914: A book of readings,* Chicago 1966). Among several general histories of the Middle East, that of Carl Brockelmann (*History of the Islamic peoples,* London 1947) has the merit of being based on first-hand use of oriental sources and orientalist literature.

THE IMPACT OF THE WEST

The processes and problems of westernization in the Middle East have formed the subject of a vast literature, of which only a few examples, dealing with general topics, can be mentioned. Robert Montagne ('The "Modern State" in Africa and Asia', in *The Cambridge Journal* v/10, July 1952, pp. 583–602) surveys the effects of the introduction of modern political institutions by the imperial powers; D. A. Rustow (*Politics and westernization in the Near East,* Princeton 1956; reprinted in Nolte, *The modern Middle East,* cited above) deals with problems of political organization and leadership resulting from westernization; H. A. R. Gibb (*Studies on the civilization of Islam,* London 1962) and G. E. von Grunebaum (*Modern Islam: the search for cultural identity,* Berkeley and Los Angeles 1962) with some problems of cultural confrontation; D. Lerner (*The passing of traditional society: modernizing the Middle East,* Glencoe Ill. 1958) with aspects of social change, particularly those concerned with the revolution in communications; C. A. O. van Nieuwenhuijze ('Contacts between Near East and West and the problems of modernization', in *Essays on unbalanced growth,* Institute of Social Studies, Series Maior X, The Hague 1962, pp. 166–99) surveys the whole problem from the viewpoint of a social scientist. Collections of papers on different aspects of the problem have been edited by B. Rivlin and J. S. Szyliowicz (*The contemporary Middle East: tradition and innovation,* New York 1965); by G. S. Métraux and F. Crouzet (*The new Asia: readings in the history of mankind,* New York 1965); by R. H. Nolte in the volume already cited and, on some contemporary problems, in a Turkish conference report, *Social aspects of economic development,* Istanbul 1964. A group of papers by various authors, edited by R. N. Frye (*Islam and the West,* The Hague 1957) deals with Islamic responses to the stimulus of westernization, in the forms of nationalism, secularism and religious modernism. A German orientalist, W. Braune (*Der islamische Orient zwischen Vergangenheit und Zukunft,* Berne-Munich 1960) has examined the moral and intellectual predicament of Islam in the modern world. Besides these, reference may be made to works dealing with specific topics and countries, as for example on Iran (A. Banani, *The modernization of Iran 1921–1941,* Stanford 1961; L. Binder, *Iran: political development in a changing society,* Berkeley and Los Angeles 1962); Turkey (B. Lewis, *The emergence of modern Turkey,* cited above; R. H. Davison, *Reform in the Ottoman Empire 1856–1876,* Princeton 1963; R. D. Robinson, *The first Turkish Republic: a case study in national development,* Cambridge Mass. 1963); Egypt (C. Issawi, *Egypt at mid-century,* London 1954; idem, *Egypt in Revolution: an economic analysis,* London 1963; Jean and Simone Lacouture, *Egypt in transition,* London 1958; J. Heyworth-Dunne, *An introduction to the history of education in modern Egypt,* London 1938); Syria-Lebanon (A. Hourani, *Syria and Lebanon,* London 1946); Israel (N. Safran, *The United States and Israel,* Cambridge Mass. 1963); Russian Empire and Soviet Union (A. G. Park, *Bolshevism in Turkestan 1917–1927,* New York 1957; R. Pierce, *Russian Central Asia 1867–1917,* Berkeley and Los Angeles 1960).

GOVERNMENT AND POLITICS

Brief, critical introductions to the politics and political institutions of the area have been written by D. A. Rustow (in G. A. Almond and James S. Coleman, ed. *The politics of the developing areas,* Princeton 1960, pp. 369–454), G. Lenczowski (in Ruth Nanda Anshen, ed. *Mid-East: World-Center, yesterday, today, and tomorrow,* New York 1956, pp. 118–72) and, more extensively, by M. Halpern (*The politics of social change in the Middle East and North Africa,* Princeton 1963). Recent trends are surveyed and explained, with documents by Hisham Sharabi (*Nationalism and Revolution in the Arab World,* Princeton 1966). Some personal impressions of Arab politics and politicians are given by H. E. Tütsch (*Facets of Arab nationalism,* Detroit 1965). Surveys of the systems of government in Middle Eastern countries have been written by M. Harari (*Government and politics of the Middle East,* Englewood Cliffs N.J. 1962) and H. Sharabi (*Governments and politics of the Middle East,* Princeton 1962). Recent developments in the area are reviewed and interpreted by H. E. Tütsch (*From Ankara to Marrakesh: Turks and Arabs in a changing world,* London 1964). Studies on individual countries include, besides those mentioned above, works on Turkey (K. H. Karpat, *Turkey's politics: the transition to a multi-party system,* Princeton 1959; W. F. Weiker, *The Turkish revolution: 1960–1961,* Washington 1963; R. E. Ward and D. A. Rustow, (editors), *Political modernization in Japan and Turkey,* Princeton 1964; F. W. Frey, *The Turkish political élite,* Cambridge Mass. 1965; D. A. Rustow, 'Turkey: the modernity of tradition', in L. W. Pye and S. Verba (editors), *Political culture and political development,* Princeton 1965, pp. 171–98); Syria (G. H. Torrey, *Syrian politics and the military 1945–1958,* Columbus Ôhio 1964; P. Seale, *The struggle for Syria, a study of post-war Arab politics 1945–1958,* London 1965); Lebanon (P. Rondot, *Les institutions politiques du Liban,* Paris 1947; Leila M. T. Meo, *Lebanon: improbable nation,* Bloomington 1965); Israel (M. H. Bernstein, *The politics of Israel: the first decade of statehood,* Princeton 1957); Iraq (M. Khadduri, *Independent Iraq: a study in Iraqi politics from 1932 to 1958,* 2nd ed. London 1960); Egypt (Anouar Abdel-Malik, *Égypte: société militaire,* Paris 1962; P. J. Vatikiotis, *The Egyptian army in politics,* Bloomington 1961; L. Binder, 'Egypt: the integrative revolution', in Pye and Verba, *Political culture,* cited above) ; Iran (D. N. Wilber, *Contemporary Iran,* London 1963; L. Binder, *Iran: political development . . . ,* cited above; J. Marlowe, *Iran: a short political guide,* London 1963). Political institutions are examined in several articles in the new edition of the *Encyclopaedia of Islam,* notably *Djam'iyya* (societies), *Djumhūriyya* (republic), *Dustūr* (constitution), *Hizb* (party), *Hukūma* (government) and *Hurriyya* (freedom). The articles on constitutions have been reprinted in a revised and amplified form in *A survey of the constitutions of the Arab and Muslim states,* Leiden 1966. Constitutional and political documents relating to Arab states are collected in Muhammad Khalil, *The Arab states and the Arab League,* 2 vols., Beirut 1962. The development of political ideas is examined by A. Hourani (*Arabic thought in the liberal age,* London 1962), N. Safran (*Egypt in search of political community: an analysis of the intellectual and political evolution of Egypt, 1804–1952,* Cambridge Mass. 1961), M. Kerr, ('Arab radical notions of democracy', in *St. Antony's Papers,* no. xvi, *Middle Eastern Affairs, no. 3,* London 1963, pp. 9–40), Ş. Mardin (*The genesis of Young Ottoman thought: a study in the modernization of Turkish political ideas,* Princeton N.J. 1962), Niyazi Berkes (*The development of secularism in Turkey,* Montreal 1964), and, in the context of recent and current events, by L. Binder (*The ideological revolution in the Middle East,* New York 1964). Communism has been examined by W. Z. Laqueur (*Communism and socialism in the Middle East,* London 1956), Arab socialism by G. Majdalany ('The Arab socialist movement', in W. Z. Laqueur, ed. *The Middle East in transition,* London 1958, pp. 337–50), by M. H. Kerr ('The emergence of a socialist ideology in Egypt', in *Middle East Journal,* xvi/2, 1962, pp. 127–44), by Takeshi Hayashi ('On Arab socialism', in *The Developing Economies,* Tokyo, ii/1, 1964, pp. 78–90), and in a series of articles and translations in the French quarterly review *Orient.* Some notes and documents on socialism in the Middle East before 1914 are given by G. Haupt and M. Sfia in *Le Mouvement Social,* no. 45, 1963, pp. 121–42. Military rule has been examined by M. Khadduri ('The role of the military in Middle East politics', in *American Political Science Review,* xlvii/2, 1953, pp. 511–24); G. M. Haddad (*Revolutions and military rule in the Middle East,* New York 1965); M. Berger (*Military élite and social change: Egypt since Napoleon,* Princeton 1960); P. J. Vatikiotis (*The Egyptian army in politics,* cited above) and in a group of papers by various authors, edited by S. N. Fisher (*The military in the Middle East: problems in society and government,* Columbus Ohio 1963).

NATIONALISM AND PATRIOTISM

Problems of Muslim and Middle Eastern nationalism have been considered in the volumes, already cited, by G. E. von Grunebaum and (edited by) R. N. Frye; by R. Hartmann (*Islam und Nationalismus,* Berlin 1948); and, within a larger context, by E. Kedourie (*Nationalism,* 2nd edition, London 1961) and R. Emerson (*From empire to nation,* Cambridge Mass. 1960). A classical statement of Arab nationalism is that of George Antonius (*The Arab awakening,* London 1938, to be read in conjunction with

Suggestions for Further Reading

W. Braune, 'Die Entwicklung des Nationalismus bei den Arabern' in R. Hartmann and H. Scheel, ed. *Beiträge zur Arabistik, Semitistik und Islamwissenschaft*, Leipzig 1944, pp. 425–38, R. Hartmann, 'Arabische politische Gesellschaften bis 1914', ibid, pp. 439–67, Sylvia G. Haim, ' "The Arab Awakening": a source for the historian?' in *Welt des Islam* n.s. ii/4, 1953, pp. 237–50 and Z. N. Zeine, *Arab-Turkish relations and the emergence of Arab nationalism*, Beirut 1958). More recent expositions include, besides the works of Hourani and Safran already cited, those of N. Z. Nuseibeh (*The ideas of Arab nationalism,* Ithaca 1956), J. M. Ahmed (*The intellectual origins of Egyptian nationalism,* London 1960), and C. Ernest Dawn ('From Ottomanism to Arabism: the origin of an ideology', in *The Review of Politics,* xxiii/3, 1961, pp. 378–400; and 'The rise of Arabism in Syria', in *Middle East Journal,* xvi/2, 1962, pp. 145–68). On some recent political aspects of pan-Arabism, reference may be made to articles by Anwar G. Chejne ('Egyptian attitudes towards pan-Arabism', in *Middle East Journal,* xi/3, 1957, pp. 253–68); M. Colombe ('La nouvelle politique arabe de la République arabe unie', in *Orient,* no. 11, 1959, pp. 13–19); and, by various authors, in the volume edited by W. Z. Laqueur, already cited. An anthology of Arab nationalist writings in English translation, with an introduction and notes, has been published by Sylvia G. Haim (*Arab nationalism,* Berkeley and Los Angeles 1962). A particular aspect of the role and function of Arab nationalism has been examined by Maxime Rodinson ('Nature et fonction des mythes dans les mouvements socio-politiques d'après deux exemples comparés: communisme marxiste et nationalisme arabe', in *Cahiers internationaux de Sociologie,* 1962, pp. 97–113). Among studies on individual nationalist writers, mention may be made of those on Muṣṭafā Kāmil (F. Steppat, 'Nationalismus und Islam bei Muṣṭafā Kāmil . . .' in *Welt des Islam,* n.s. iv/4, 1956, pp. 241–341), on Kawākibī (N. Tapiero, *Les idées reformistes d'al-Kawâkibî,* Paris 1956; Sylvia G. Haim, 'Alfieri and al-Kawākibī, in *Oriente Moderno,* xxxiv, 1954, pp. 321–34; idem, 'Blunt and al-Kawākibī, in *Oriente Moderno,* xxxv, 1955, pp. 132–43). The religious sources of Zionism have been examined by M. Buber (*Israel and Palestine: the history of an idea,* London 1952); the political development of the movement by I. Cohen (*A short history of Zionism,* London 1951) and B. Halpern (*The idea of a Jewish state,* Cambridge Mass. 1960). An anthology of Zionist texts has been edited and presented by A. Hertzberg (*The Zionist idea,* New York 1960). Other Middle

Eastern nationalisms have received far less attention. Accounts of Turkish nationalism have been given by E. Rossi ('Dall' Impero ottomano alla Repubblica di Turchia: origine e sviluppi del nazionalismo turco sotto l'aspetto politico-culturale', in *Oriente Moderno*, xxiii, 1943, pp. 359–88) and by N. Berkes, B. Lewis, and Ş. Mardin, in the works cited above. Some of the writings of Ziya Gökalp have been translated and presented by Niyazi Berkes (*Turkish nationalism and western civilization*, London 1959); the same writer forms the subject of a monograph by U. Heyd (*The foundations of Turkish nationalism*, London 1950). A view of recent Persian nationalism is given by R. W. Cottam (*Nationalism in Iran*, Pittsburgh 1964); for further discussions, besides the works of Avery, Frye, Banani and Binder already cited, reference may be made to monographic articles by Nikki R. Keddie ('Religion and irreligion in early Iranian nationalism', in *Comparative Studies in Society and History*, iv/3, 1962, pp. 265–95) and Ann K. S. Lambton ('Secret societies and the Persian Revolution of 1905–6' in *St. Antony's Papers*, no. 4, *Middle Eastern Affairs no. I*, London 1958, pp. 43–60, and 'Persian political societies 1906–11', in *St. Antony's Papers*, no. xvi, *Middle Eastern Affairs no. 3*, London 1963, pp. 41–89). Nationalism among the Muslim peoples of the Soviet Union has been discussed by A. Bennigsen and C. Quelquejay (*Histoire des mouvements nationaux chez les musulmans de Russie—le sultangaliévisme au Tatarstan*, Paris—The Hague 1960; *La presse et le mouvement national chez les musulmans de Russie avant 1920*, Paris—The Hague 1964); A. Zenkovsky (*Pan-Turkism and Islam in Russia*, Cambridge Mass. 1960); C. W. Hostler (*Turkism and the Soviets*, London 1957); Baymirza Hayit (*Turkestan im zwanzigsten Jahrhundert*, Darmstadt 1956), and the works already cited on Central Asia.

ISLAM

The role of Islam in the life, thought and politics of the Islamic peoples is considered in many of the works cited above, notably those of Berkes, Binder, Braune, Frye, Gibb, Hourani, Lewis, Safran and von Grunebaum. A brief historical introduction to Islam has been translated into English from the French of D. Sourdel (*Islam*, New York 1962). An elementary introduction to Islam, past and present, is provided by P. Rondot (*L'Islam*, Paris 1965). More specifically concerned with the evolution of religious thought and doctrines are H. A. R. Gibb (*Mohammedanism, an historical survey*, revised ed. London 1961); M. Guidi

Suggestions for Further Reading

('Storia della religione dell'Islam' in P. Tacchi-Venturi, *Storia delle Religioni*, ii, Turin, 1936, pp. 229–359), and A. Bausani ('Religione islamica' in *Le civiltà dell'Oriente*, iii, Rome 1958, pp. 293–412). A general survey of the Islamic world, its history, institutions, religion, and culture has been edited by Father F. M. Pareja and published in Italian (*Islamologia*, Rome 1951), Spanish (*Islamología*, 2 vols., Madrid 1952–54) and French (*Islamologie*, Beirut 1964), but not English. Various aspects of Islamic religion and civilization are examined in a volume of essays edited by Sir Thomas Arnold and Alfred Guillaume (*The legacy of Islam*, Oxford 1931). Notable among these is the contribution on 'Law and Society' by David de Santillana. A fuller discussion of Islamic political and constitutional ideas, by the same author, will be found in the introductory chapters to his *Istituzioni di diritto musulmano malichita, con riguardo anche al sistema sciafiita*, i, Rome 1926. The development of Islamic law is also discussed by J. Schacht (*An introduction to Islamic law*, Oxford 1964); N. J. Coulson (*A history of Islamic law*, Edinburgh 1964); G. H. Bousquet (*Du droit musulman et de son application effective dans le monde*, Algiers 1949); J. N. D. Anderson (*Islamic law in the modern world*, London 1959); and in the papers edited by M. Khadduri and H. J. Liebesny (*Law in the Middle East*, i, *Origin and development of Islamic law*, Washington 1955). The political and social attitudes and problems of the Islamic community have been examined by L. Gardet (*La cité musulmane: vie sociale et politique*, Paris 1954); the role of Islam in political life by E. I. J. Rosenthal (*Islam in the modern national state*, Cambridge 1965), and in a collection of papers edited by J. Harris Proctor (*Islam and international relations*, New York 1965); the problems and movements of contemporary Islam by W. Cantwell Smith (*Islam in modern history*, Princeton 1957), P. Rondot (*L'Islam et les musulmans d'aujourd'hui*, 2 vols., revised ed. Paris 1965), and R. Paret (editor, *Die Welt des Islam und die Gegenwart*, Stuttgart 1961) as well as in the works of W. Braune and G. E. von Grunebaum already cited. Modern religious movements have been examined by H. A. R. Gibb (*Modern trends in Islam*, Chicago 1947) and, more briefly, by I. Goldziher (chapter VI of his *Vorlesungen über den Islam*, Heidelberg 1910; also available in French, Hungarian, Russian, Arabic and Hebrew, but not English). Further information will be found in the volume of essays edited by H. A. R. Gibb (*Whither Islam? A survey of modern movements in the Muslim world*, London 1932); more recent trends have been discussed by P. J. Vatikiotis and G. Makdisi ('Recent developments in Islam', in P. W. Thayer, *Tensions in the Middle East*, Baltimore 1958) and K. Cragg (*Counsels in contemporary Islam*, Edinburgh 1965). Special aspects and movements are examined in monographic studies by G. E. von Grunebaum (*Islam: essays in the nature and growth of a cultural tradition*, London 1955); H. Laoust ('Le réformisme orthodoxe des Salafiyya et les caractères généraux de son orientation actuelle', in *Revue des études islamiques*, 1932, pp. 175–224, and 'Le reformisme musulman dans la littérature arabe contemporaine', in *Orient*, no. 10, 1959, pp. 81–107); C. C. Adams (*Islam and modernism in Egypt*, London 1933); I. M. Husaini (*The Moslem Brethren*, Beirut 1956); Christina Phelps Harris (*Nationalism and revolution in Egypt: the role of the Muslim Brotherhood*, The Hague 1964); J. H. Dunne (*Religious and political trends in modern Egypt*, Washington 1950); E. Sarkisyanz (*Russland und der Messianismus des Orients*, Tübingen 1955); P. J. Vatikiotis ('Muhammad 'Abduh and the quest for a Muslim humanism' in *Arabica* iv/1, 1957, pp. 55–72); E. Kedourie (*Afghānī and 'Abduh: an essay on religious unbelief and political activisim in modern Islam*, London 1966); Nikki R. Keddie ('Afghani in Afghanistan', in *Middle Eastern Studies*, i, 1965, 322–49), and Ch. Lemercier-Quelquejay ('Un réformateur tatar au XIX⁰ siècle; 'Abdul Qajjum al-Nasyri,' in *Cahiers du Monde russe et soviétique*, iv, 1963, pp. 117–42). Excerpts from the writings of Jamāl al-Dīn al-Afghānī have been translated into French by M. Colombe ('Pages choisies de Djamal al-din al-Afghani', in *Orient*, no. 21, 1962, pp. 87–115; no. 22, 1962, pp. 125–59; no. 23, 1962, pp. 169–98; no. 24, 1962, pp. 125–51).

INTERNATIONAL RELATIONS

The interests and policies of the powers in the Middle East have been examined, from different points of view, by many authors, among them J. C. Campbell (*Defense of the Middle East*, New York 1958); Sir Reader Bullard (*Britain and the Middle East from the earliest times to 1963*, London 1964); G. Lenczowski (*The Middle East in world affairs*, 2nd ed. Ithaca N.Y. 1956); W. Z. Laqueur (*The Soviet Union and the Middle East*, London 1959); I. Spector (*The Soviet Union and the Muslim world 1917–1958*, Seattle 1959); J. C. Hurewitz (*Middle East dilemmas: the background of United States policy*, New York 1953); J. Marlowe (*Arab nationalism and British imperialism*, London

Suggestions for Further Reading

1961); G. E. Kirk (*Contemporary Arab politics: a concise history*, New York 1961); Pierre Rondot (*The changing patterns of the Middle East*, revised ed., New York 1962); C. D. Cremeans (*The Arabs and the world: Nasser's Arab nationalist policy*, New York 1963); E. Kedourie (*England and the Middle East: the destruction of the Ottoman Empire 1914–1921*, London 1956); Elizabeth Monroe (*Britain's moment in the Middle East 1914–1956*, London 1963); M. A. Fitzsimons (*Empire by treaty: Britain and the Middle East in the twentieth century*, Notre Dame 1964); J. A. de Novo (*American interests and policies in the Middle East 1900–1939*, Minneapolis 1964); W. R. Polk (*The United States and the Arab world*, Cambridge Mass. 1965); Georgiana G. Stevens (ed., *The United States and the Middle East*, Englewood Cliffs 1964); G. Lenczowski (*Russia and the west in Iran 1918–1948*, Ithaca N.Y. 1949).Shorter studies by various authors will be found in the St. Antony's Papers (*Middle Eastern Affairs*, numbers 1–4, London 1958, 1961, 1963, 1965) and in the volumes edited by P. W. Thayer (cited above), W. Z. Laqueur (*The Middle East in transition*, London 1958) and R. C. Macridis (*Foreign policy in world politics*, 2nd ed. Englewood Cliffs N.J. 1962). Inter-Arab relations are discussed by M. Kerr (*The Arab cold war 1958–1964*, London 1965) and R. W. MacDonald (*The league of Arab states*, Princeton 1965); a documentary record is provided by Muhammad Khalil (*The Arab states and the Arab league*, vol. ii, Beirut 1962). The beginnings of Middle Eastern diplomacy are discussed by J. C. Hurewitz ('Ottoman diplomacy and the European state system', in *Middle East Journal*, xv, 1961, pp. 141–52), T. Naff ('Reform and the conduct of Ottoman diplomacy in the reign of Selim III 1789–1807', in *Journal of the American Oriental Society*, lxxxiii, 1963, pp. 295–315), and in the *Encyclopaedia of Islam*, article *Elči*. Collections of documents have been edited by J. C. Hurewitz (*Diplomacy in the Near and Middle East*, 2 vols., Princeton 1956); K. Strupp (*Ausgewählte diplomatische Aktenstücke zur orientalischen Frage*, Gotha 1916); A. Giannini (*Documenti per la storia della pace orientale*, Rome 1933); and E. Rossi (*Documenti sull'origine e gli sviluppi della questione araba: 1875–1944*, Rome 1944). The Middle Eastern settlements following the First World War are chronicled and examined in the work edited by H. M. V. Temperley (*A history of the peace conference in Paris*, vi, London 1924). Following upon this, a presentation and interpretation of events since 1920 will be found in the volumes of the *Survey of International Affairs*, published by the Royal Institute of International Affairs, London, with documents in the parallel series of *Documents on International Affairs*. Discussions of recent and current events will be found in the journals and surveys devoted to the Middle East (*Middle Eastern Affairs*, New York; *Middle East Journal*, Washington; *Middle East Record*, London-Jerusalem; *Middle Eastern Studies*, London; *Chronology of Arab politics* and *Arab Political Documents*, Beirut; *Cahiers de l'Orient Contemporain*, Paris; *Orient*, Paris; *Welt des Islam*, Leiden; *Oriente Moderno*, Rome, etc.).

BIBLIOGRAPHY

The above represents only a very brief selection from the vast literature on the Middle East—even from that small fragment of it that is worth serious attention. Further bibliographical guidance may be found in H. B. Sharabi, *A handbook on the contemporary Middle East*, Washington 1956; R. Ettinghausen, *A selected and annotated bibliography of books and periodicals in western languages dealing with the Near and Middle East, with special emphasis on medieval and modern times*, Washington 1954; R. H. Davison, *The Near and Middle East: an introduction to history and bibliography*, Washington 1959; idem, 'The Middle East since 1450', in the American Historical Association's *Guide to historical literature*, New York 1961, pp. 218–32. Soviet publications are surveyed in *Mizan*, London. Classified bibliographies of articles in periodicals will be found in J. D. Pearson, *Index Islamicus 1906–1955*, Cambridge 1958; idem, *Index Islamicus Supplement 1956–1960*, Cambridge 1962; in *A selected bibliography of articles dealing with the Middle East*, 3 parts, Jerusalem 1954–1959, and in the surveys of periodical literature appearing in *Middle East Journal*.

INDEX

Arab and Persian names and terms are transcribed in accordance with the system customary among orientalists. Turkish names are given in a slightly modified form of the official Turkish orthography.